Just Joking

JUMBO

2

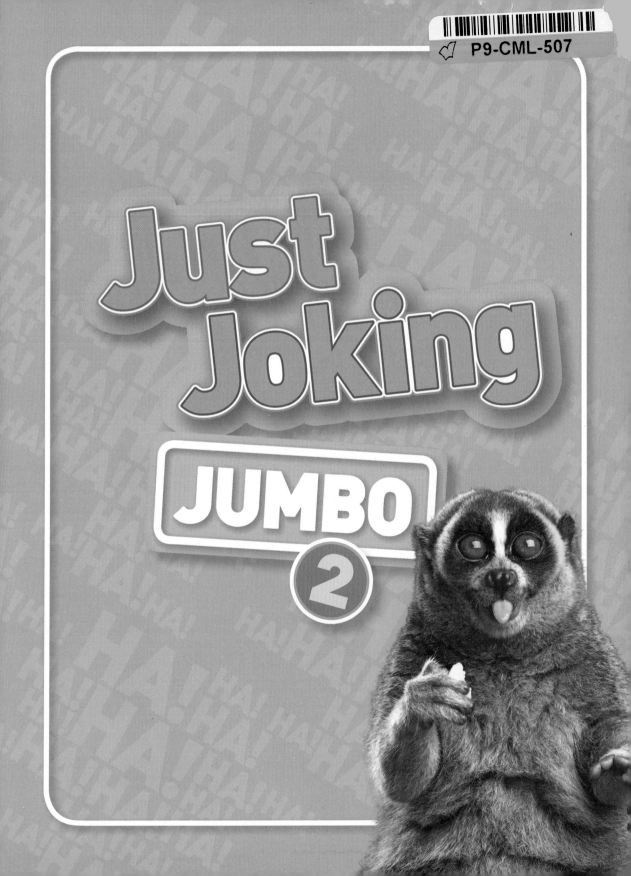

Just Joking

JUMBO 2

1,000
Giant Jokes &
1,000 Funny Photos
Add Up to
Big Laughs

Rosie
Gowsell
Pattison

NATIONAL GEOGRAPHIC
WASHINGTON, D.C.

Contents

Tokay geckos use
sticky hairlike
structures on their
toes to walk up walls.

CHAPTER 1

Preposterous Pets

6

Don't be shy about talking to your pooch; the average pup understands about 160 words. Good dog!

KNOCK, KNOCK.

Who's there?

Collie.

Collie who?

Collie you when it's time to take the dogs for a walk.

What has **armor**, but doesn't fight and is **always home** when on the move?

A turtle.

Q What do you get if you cross a puppy and a frog?

A A dog that can lick you from the other side of the yard.

BIRD: Why are you standing at the bus stop? **FROG:** Because my car got toad.

Q How do **hedgehogs** hug each other?

A Very, very carefully.

8

Q What's an **Irish setter's** favorite holiday?

A St. Pawtrick's Day.

JEFF: What kind of dog finds rare artifacts?
ERIN: A bark-eologist.
JEFF: How does he find them?
ERIN: He digs them up.

Q Where do the royal corgis live?

A In Barkingham Palace.

Q Why are **kittens** good at **sports?**

A Because they are very cat-hletic.

Q How do you stop a canary from calling?

A Take away its cell phone.

9

DID SOMEONE SAY "CHEESE"?

Q Where do rabbits go after they get married?

A On their bunnymoon.

JULIA: I was going to teach my turtle to ride a bike but changed my mind.
CATHIE: Why?
JULIA: Because he doesn't have a thumb to ring the bell.

Q Why are fish terrible tennis players?

A They don't like getting close to the net.

Q What do you get if you cross a **giraffe** and a **hedgehog?**

A A six-foot-long toothbrush.

Q What kind of dog doesn't bark?

A A hush puppy.

Q Why did the ferret say "moo"?

A It was learning a new language.

Q Why did the **turtle** feel sorry for the **frog?**

A Because he thought the frog was homeless.

Q Why don't cats like dog jokes?

A Because they are pawful.

10

KNOCK, KNOCK.

Who's there?

Kitten.

Kitten who?

I packed everything but the kitten sink for our vacation!

Adult cats don't meow to each other. They only meow to communicate with humans.

KNOCK, KNOCK.

Who's there?
Whisker.
Whisker who?
Is Anne ready? I'm going to whisker away on a special trip.

Guinea pigs jump up and down when they are happy. This is often called popcorning.

"I SAID, "DO YOU WANT TO COME OUT AND PLAY?""

Q Why don't cats like riddles?

A They find them purr-plexing.

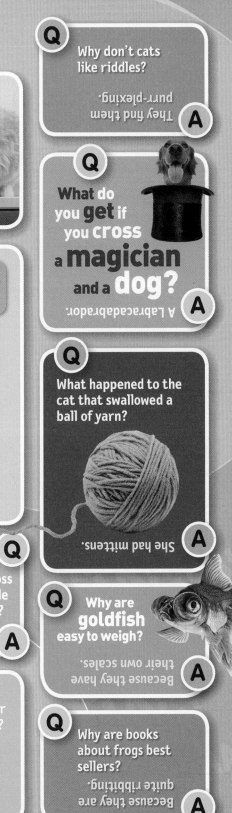

Q What do you **get** if you **cross** a **magician** and a **dog**?

A A Labracadabrador.

LAUGHABLE LIST

FAVORITE DOG MOVIES:

☐ *Mary Puppins*
☐ *Bichon and the Beast*
☐ *Squeaky Toy Story*
☐ *Kung Fu Poodle*
☐ *Wizard of Paws*
☐ *Corgi With a Chance of Meatballs*

Q What happened to the cat that swallowed a ball of yarn?

A She had mittens.

Q What do you get if you cross a carnival ride and a weasel?

A A ferret wheel.

Q Why are **goldfish** easy to weigh?

A Because they have their own scales.

STEPHEN: Are you going to teach your dog to play soccer?
ANNA: Of course not, he's a boxer!

Q Why are books about frogs best sellers?

A Because they are quite ribbiting.

13

SAY WHAT?

NAME Boss

FAVORITE ACTIVITY
Raiding the company fridge

FAVORITE TOY
Rubber-band balls

PET PEEVE
Forgetting my computer paws-word

The United States has the highest population of pet pooches. There are more than 70 million dogs living in the country.

THIS JOB MAKES ME DOGGONE TIRED.

WHEN I FETCHED THE STICK, I DIDN'T KNOW I'D BECOME THE BRANCH MANAGER!

I'M HAVING A RUFF TIME WITH THIS COMPUTER.

IF I DON'T GET THIS WORK DONE, I'LL JUST EAT IT.

MY BOSS IS HOUNDING ME TO FINISH THIS REPORT.

Q Why do cats like going to spas?

They enjoy being paw-purred.

A

Q What do cats put in their soft drinks?

Mice cubes.

A

RIDDLE ME THIS

Which animal wears a coat in the winter and pants in the summer?

A dog.

IT'S ABOUT TIME SOMEONE LET THE CAT OUT OF THE BAG!

Q What's the difference between a dog and a marine biologist?

One wags a tail and the other tags a whale.

A

JOSH: Oh no! My bird escaped its cage!

DYLAN: Looks like it used a crow-bar to escape.

Did you know that **cats** were kept as pets in **ancient Egypt?**

They were considered sacred and associated with Bastet, a goddess who was half woman, half cat.

TONGUE TWISTER!

Say this fast three times:

A slimy snake slithered south to the sandy Sahara.

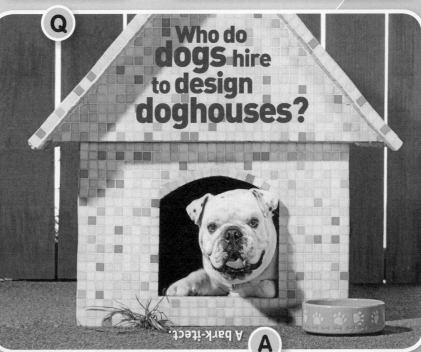

POLICE OFFICER: We caught your dog chasing people on bikes.

DOG OWNER: That's impossible, my dog doesn't even own a bike.

Q

Who do **dogs** hire to **design doghouses?**

A bark-itect.

A

A BOY WALKS INTO A LIBRARY AND CHECKS OUT A BOOK.

Ten minutes later he returns it and gets another.

Ten minutes later he enters the library again, returns the second book, and takes out a third. The librarian becomes suspicious and follows the boy outside where he sees him talking to his pet frog.

The boy shows the book to the frog and says, "Okay, I'm getting tired of this. How about this book?"

And the frog replies, "Reddit, reddit."

KNOCK, KNOCK.

Who's there?

Cook.

Cook who?

Stop making bird noises and open the door!

A parakeet's heart beats more than 300 times a minute.

What part of a **bird isn't** in the **sky** and can **swim without** getting **wet**?

The bird's shadow.

Q What do you get if you cross a turtle and a hedgehog?

A A slowpoke.

Q Where do mice park their boats?

A At the hickory dickory dock.

BUS DRIVER: Where to?
FROG: I'm heading down to the pond. Mind if I catch a ride?
BUS DRIVER: Hop on!

Q What do cats listen to on their music players?

A Mew-sic.

Q What do rabbit surgeons perform?

A Hop-erations.

Q Why do Labradors like to wear hats?

A Because they look quite fetching.

Q What do you call **a dog standing in the snow?**

A A chill dog.

Q Why did the fish get embarrassed?

A Because it saw the ocean's bottom.

21

Goldfish don't have eyelids. That's why they are always staring at you.

KNOCK, KNOCK.

Who's there?
Chicken.
Chicken who?
I'd like to chicken to my room, please.

I'M A PARTY ANIMAL!

Q What is a **cat's** favorite **TV show?**

A Claw and Order.

Q What do you call a pet snake that can't sit still?

A Viper active.

Q Why did the teacher bring birdseed to class?

A She had a parrot-teacher conference.

Q What do you call a guinea pig with three eyes?

A Guinea piiig.

Q What kind of car do kittens drive?

A Cat-illacs.

Q What did the **schnauzer** say to the **hot dog bun?**

A "Are you a pure bred?"

PARAKEET 1: Is it hot out today?
PARAKEET 2: I didn't check the feather forecast.

Q How do **rabbits** travel?

A By hare-plane.

23

Q

What do you call an extremely happy feline?

Q What do you get if you cross a pig and a parrot?

A A bird who hogs the conversation.

TEACHER: If I give you two cats and then another two cats, how many do you have?
SAM: Five.
TEACHER: How did you get five as an answer?
SAM: Because I already have a pet cat at home.

CAN YOU TURN THE HEAT UP?

CAN YOU TURN THE AIR-CONDITIONING ON?

Q What do you call a dog on a tanning bed?

SUN SCREEN
25 SPF

A A hot dog.

TONGUE TWISTER!

Say this fast three times:

Feathered finches flinch.

A giddy cat. **A**

SHEEPDOG: All 40 sheep are in the pen.
FARMER: But we only have 38 sheep.
SHEEPDOG: I know, but I rounded them up.

Did you know that **hairless dogs** have a **genetic defect** that causes their naked appearance?

These bare beauties are also completely odorless.

RIDDLE ✹ ✹ ME THIS

I'm **alive** without **air.** I'm always **drinking** but **never** thirsty. What am I?

A fish.

Q How do schnauzers celebrate the Fourth of July?

A They have a bark-becue.

Q

What do **dogs** eat while watching movies?

Pup-corn. **A**

25

NAME Mew-lissa

FAVORITE ACTIVITY Meow-deling new fashions

DAILY GOALS Tabby the best dressed

PET PEEVE Smelly purr-fume

I THINK MY NEW LOOK IS GETTING A PAWSITIVE REACTION.

LOOKIN' GOOD, FELINE GOOD.

CATITUDE IS EVERYTHING.

A cat's nose has a unique pattern on it that is just as distinct as a human fingerprint.

MEOW YOU DOIN'?

KNOCK, KNOCK.

Who's there?
Litter.
Litter who?
I litter-ally have nothing fun to wear.

Iguanas use their large tails to "punch" their attackers.

KNOCK, KNOCK.

Who's there?
Iguana.
Iguana who?
Iguana come inside!

If a **cat** can **jump** five feet high, why **can't** it jump **through** a window that is only **three feet high?**

The window is closed.

I FEEL LIKE I SHOULD BE THERE BY NOW. DID I PASS THE WATER BOTTLE ALREADY?

Q What did the frog order at the fast-food restaurant?

A hoppy meal and flies. **A**

Q Why do Shar-Peis have so many wrinkles?

Because they're hard to iron. **A**

Q Where does a poodle leave its car?

In the barking lot. **A**

Q What do you get if you cross a **dog** and a **vegetable?**

A pug-tato. **A**

Q When is it bad luck to see a black cat?

When you're a mouse. **A**

TING: Did you see the famous turtle over there?
LI: Wow, a real shell-ebrity!

Q What do you call a rodent with good aim?

Accu-rat. **A**

29

KNOCK, KNOCK.

Who's there?
Goat.
Goat who?
Goat to go, we're running late!

Goats can be taught to respond to their names and come when they are called.

30

WILL: Did you hear about the German shepherd on the hockey team?
KATE: He got a two-minute penalty for ruffing.

Q Why did the mother cat move her kittens away from the park?

A She didn't want to get caught littering.

Q Why is turtle wax so expensive?

A Because they have such small ears.

LAUGHABLE LIST

CAT EMPLOYMENT OPPORTUNITIES:

☐ Gravity tester (usually with your cup of cocoa)

☐ Keyboard warmer (while you are trying to use the computer)

☐ Fabric strength investigator (down the side of the couch)

☐ Feline scarf (Who needs to breathe?)

☐ Late-night opera singer (Why sleep when you can listen to a free live performance?)

POODLE: What movie do you want to watch?
PUG: *Bark to the Future*?
POODLE: I'd rather watch something scary.
PUG: How about *Jurassic Bark*?

Q How do **dogs** listen to **music**?

A On their subwoofers.

Q What do you give a dog with a fever?

A Mustard— it's the best thing for a hot dog.

SNAKE 1: Are we venomous?
SNAKE 2: I don't know, why?
SNAKE 1: Because I just bit my lip.

31

LOL PETS

The **LATIN NAME** name for **FERRET**, *Mustela putorius furo*, means "**smelly little thief.**"

DUKE, a Great Pyrenees, **was elected** **MAYOR** of **a Minnesota, U.S.A.,** town for **three terms.**

Rats LAUGH **and jump when they** **are** tickled.

★ **LOST** ★

MADE A SLOW ESCAPE

A family in **Brazil** lost **their pet** **tortoise** **and found it** **30 YEARS** **LATER** **still** living **in** **their** house!

COSMO, AN **AFRICAN GRAY PARROT,** KNOWS **950 WORDS** AND TELLS **JOKES** TO HER OWNER FOR **PEANUTS.**

JUST ANOTHER DAY IN PARROT-DISE!

Silly Science & Terrific Technology

The first known robot was a steam-powered bird created more than 2,300 years ago.

KNOCK, KNOCK.

Who's there?
Neon.
Neon who?
I fell and hurt my neon the pavement.

OH, GEAR! DID YOU WRENCH IT?

35

LAUGHABLE LIST

SIGNS YOU HAVE AN OLD COMPUTER:

- ☐ You have to crank a handle to start it.
- ☐ The screen is made by Etch-A-Sketch.
- ☐ It's connected to the Internet by a piece of string and a tin can.
- ☐ Your messaging app is a carrier pigeon.

Q Why can't you trust graph paper?

A Because it's always plotting something.

RIZZO:
Hey, did you read that new book about helium?
SHERMAN:
Sure did, I couldn't put it down!

Q What do you get if you cross a soft drink and a robot?

A A can-droid.

Q Why did the **computer** keep **sneezing?**

A It had a virus.

Q What kind of snake is good at math?

$$\sqrt{4}=2$$

A An adder.

36

Q

What do you get if you cross baking soda and an android?

A A dough-bot.

TONGUE TWISTER!

Say this fast three times:

Red bulb. Blue bulb.

I PREFER A COMPUTER WITH A MOUSE ...

Did you know that **Brazil** uses **cat face emojis** more than any other country in the **world?**

The cat with heart eyes is used the most of all the cat faces.

Q

What do you get if you cross a computer and a dairy product?

A Mac and cheese.

37

Q What did Earth say to the other planets?

A "You guys have no life."

Q What do you get if you cross helium and a monkey?

A A hot-air baboon.

You can **enter**, but you **can't come in**. I can **give you space**, but no room. I have **keys**, but **no lock**. **What am I?**

A computer keyboard.

Q What does a robot use to shave?

A A laser blade.

CATHIE: I couldn't find the escape key on my computer.
DOUG: Did you get angry?
CATHIE: I lost control!

Ctrl   Cmd   Alt

Q Why did the germ cross the microscope?

A To get to the other slide.

Q Why was the computer tired when it got home?

A Because it had a hard drive.

HEY, THERE'S FREE WI-FI IN HERE!

AND THE RENT IS SO CHEEP!

ELECTRICIAN'S BOSS: Wire you insulate?
ELECTRICIAN: Watt's it to you?

Scientists in the United States have created a huge touch screen for dolphins. The dolphins use apps to communicate with researchers and play games.

KNOCK, KNOCK.

Who's there?
Norma Lee.
Norma Lee who?
Norma Lee I don't get science jokes.

KNOCK, KNOCK.

Who's there?
Mitosis.
Mitosis who?
Mitosis cold, can I borrow some socks?

A zebra's stripes may help it camouflage itself, but the black and white stripes on a rocket are used to increase its visibility during a launch.

Q Why did the **polar bear** call **tech support** from the North Pole?

A Because his computer was frozen.

Q What do you call a doctor that fixes websites?

A A URL-ologist.

Q What do you get if you cross a sheep and a hard drive?

A Computer ram.

Q What makes an astronaut's dog itchy?

A Lunar-ticks.

Q Why do computer programmers have terrible table manners?

A Because they take mega-bites.

Q Why did the **kid** sleep on a **battery**?

A She needed a power nap.

KYLIE: The light in here is bad.
JORJA: Maybe you should send it to prism.

Q Why shouldn't you let a skunk set up your Wi-Fi network?

A Because the service will stink.

Q Why did the robot cross the road?

A Because it was programmed by the chicken.

41

SAY WHAT?

NAME Bunsen

FAVORITE ACTIVITY
Hiding under the periodic table

FAVORITE TOY
Safety glasses

PET PEEVE
Over reactions

I ENJOY CHEMISTRY JOKES PERIODICALLY.

I HAVE ALL THE SOLUTIONS!

NEVER TRUST AN ATOM— THEY MAKE UP EVERYTHING.

I HAVE A LOT IN COMMON WITH MY COMPUTER ... WE BOTH HAVE MEGA-BITES!

SOLID, LIQUID, GAS ... THEY ALL MATTER.

Caimans are better suited for swimming than walking. They use their powerful tails to propel themselves through water.

KNOCK, KNOCK.

Who's there?

Data.

Data who?

Data pizza I smell? I sure am hungry!

What happens once in a minute, twice in a moment, but never in a thousand years?

The letter m.

Q What happened when the chemist tried to tell a joke?

A She didn't get a reaction.

TONY: Why did you put glasses on your cell phone?
LOUISE: Because it lost its contacts.

Did you know that **dogs** can be trained to alert **type 1 diabetics** when their blood sugar is low?

These detection dogs are specially trained to sniff out chemical changes in the body that happen when glucose levels drop.

YES, I'M A SCIENTIST ... I BET YOU WERE EXPECTING A LAB.

ASTRONOMER 1: What a beautiful sunset!
ASTRONOMER 2: Yeah, the Earth's rotation really makes my day.

Q What kind of shot do you give a sick car engine?

A A fuel injection.

Q Why couldn't the research assistant experiment with plants?

A Because he hadn't botany.

Q Why don't **computer programmers** like nature?

A There's too many bugs.

45

ONE DAY IN ROBOTICS CLASS, the teacher asked for a group of volunteers to test a batch of new robots. Four friends raised their hands. The teacher explained the plan: "Callie, you are operator one, Alex is operator two, Ling is operator three, and Rowan is operator four." They all grabbed their remote controls and got ready.

"These four robots are incredibly strong, and we are going to use them to carry this table across the room, but you MUST all move the robots together so we don't drop it," she said.

"Remember," the teacher said, "it is EXTREMELY important that all four of you hit the button on your remotes to move the robots forward at the same time, got it?"

"Got it!" the four friends replied. "Okay, kids," the teacher said. "Ready? One, two, three—go!" Everyone but Rowan pressed the button to move their robots forward. Suddenly, there was a loud crash, and the robots and the table collapsed into a jumbled, broken pile.

"Rowan!" the robotics teacher yelled. "Why didn't you move your robot?"

Rowan replied, "Because my number is four!"

KNOCK, KNOCK.

Who's there?

Art.

Art who?

Art2-D2.

Chimpanzees are one of the few animal species that make and use tools. They dig for grubs with sticks, smash open nuts with rocks, and even use leaves as sponges to soak up drinking water.

RIDDLE ME THIS

What has **four fingers** and a thumb, gives you a **hand** in the lab, but **can't** pick up anything?

A rubber glove.

Q Why did the robot take a vacation?

A To recharge its batteries.

Q Why couldn't the computer take off its baseball hat?

A Because the caps lock was on.

Q What do you do with a **sick chemist**?

A Helium and hope you curium so you don't have to barium.

Q What do scientists use for breath freshener?

A Experi-mints.

Q How did the rocket lose its job at NASA?

A It was fired.

Q Why was there **thunder** and **lightning** in the lab?

A Because the scientists were brainstorming.

I'M THE NASTIEST COMPUTER BUG AROUND!

ROBOT: Can you help me loosen up? My neck is so stiff.
MASSAGE THERAPIST: Sure, I'll go get my screwdriver.

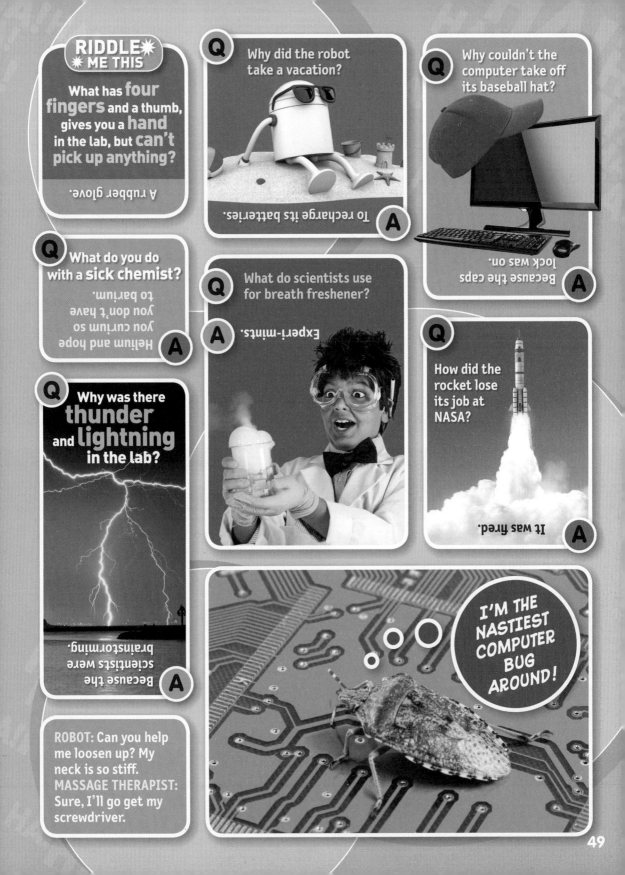

49

KNOCK, KNOCK.

Who's there?
Wire.
Wire who?
Wire you asking?
I just told you.

Q What do you get if you cross a robot and a gardener?

A Cutting-hedge technology.

COMPUTER 1: Can I borrow five dollars?
COMPUTER 2: Sorry, I used all my cache.

Q What kind of **garden** does a **droid** plant?

A A bot-tanical garden.

The cassowary, a large bird, has a long spike on each foot that it uses to defend itself.

EARS UP FOR A BETTER SIGNAL ... CAN YOU HEAR ME NOW?

LARISSA: I hear our science teacher is a vampire.
DYLAN: What?
LARISSA: She'll probably give us lots of blood tests.

Q What did the digital watch say to the grandfather clock?

A "Look, Pop! No hands!"

Q Why **couldn't** the **computer programmer sleep** at night?

A He had too much Java.

51

Q What do you call **dental x-rays?**

A Tooth pics.

Q How do **computers cool off?**

A They open windows.

VERY FUNNY, GUYS. WHO CHANGED MY SCREEN SAVER?

CHEMISTRY TEACHER: Who can tell me when the boiling point is reached?
STUDENT: When my mom sees my report card.

Q Why didn't the **computer talk** to its parents **about work?**

A Because it makes its mother board.

Q What's a computer's favorite kind of dance?

A Disk-o.

Q What do you call it when your **fingers** are **too cold** to **text properly?**

A Typo-thermia.

Did you know that **toque macaque monkeys** can have tails up to **24 inches** (61 cm) long?

These monkeys are named for their patches of hair that resemble brimless hats, called toques.

RIDDLE ✹ ✹ ME THIS

What starts out **tall**, but the **longer** it stands, the **shorter** it grows?

A candle.

ROBOT: You always make me so angry!
LAB TECH: I know how to push your buttons.

SAY WHAT?

NAME Zippy

FAVORITE ACTIVITY
Trying to remember my password

FAVORITE FOOD
Micro-chips

PET PEEVE
Caps lock

IF AT FIRST YOU DON'T SUCCEED, CALL IT VERSION 1.0.

KNOCK, KNOCK.

Who's there?

Ida.

Ida who?

Ida emailed but I have no Wi-Fi connection.

IS THE INTERNET SLOW TODAY, OR IS IT JUST ME?

55

Bomb detection dogs are trained to smell the chemical components, or ingredients, that make up explosives.

KNOCK, KNOCK.

Who's there?
Barium.
Barium who?
Barium in the sand at the beach.

Q What do computers **eat** for a snack?

A Microchips.

Q If there is H_2O on the inside of the fire hydrant, what is on the outside?

A K9P.

Q What kind of math does a bird do?

A Owl-gebra.

Q What is the first thing the lumberjack did with his new computer?

A He logged in.

Q Why are chemists great at solving problems?

A Because they have all the solutions.

SCIENCE TEACHER: I'd like to have a large whiteboard installed in my classroom.

PRINCIPAL: Sure, but what's so great about whiteboards?

SCIENCE TEACHER: They're remarkable!

Q How do **cars greet** each other?

A With their hi-beams.

Q What do computers do on first dates?

A Grab a byte.

Q How can you tell if a **cat** has been using your **computer?**

A There's teeth marks on your mouse.

KNOCK, KNOCK.

Who's there?

Argon.

Argon who?

All of my good jokes argon.

Shetland ponies are only about 42 inches (107 cm) tall.

Q What is the most important rule in a chemistry lab?

A Don't lick the spoon.

Q Did you hear about the wooden car with the wooden engine?

A It wooden go.

Q What did the biologist buy at the high-end boutique?

A Designer genes.

SCIENTIST: I'm thinking about getting a dog. Any suggestions?
ASSISTANT: How about a Lab?

RIDDLE ME THIS

If an **electric train** is traveling **east,** but there is a strong wind from the **west,** which way will the **smoke** from the train blow?

Electric trains don't produce smoke.

Q What **do you get if you cross a lifeguard** and a **computer?**

A A screen saver.

Q How do locomotives hear?

A With their engine-ears.

Q What did one **magnet** say to the **other?**

A I find you very attractive.

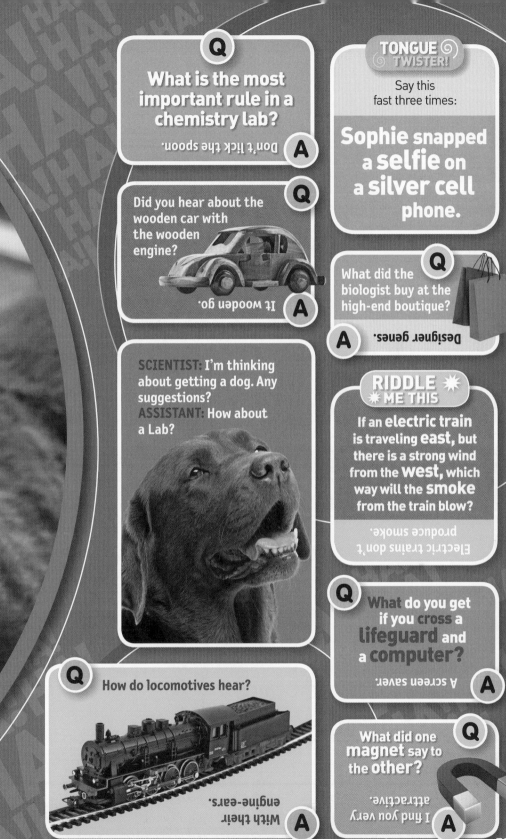

LOL

SCIENCE & TECHNOLOGY

A group of **programmers** have created a **COMPUTER CODE** that can "write" a 50,000 word novel.

In 2015, the Oxford Dictionary's **WORD** of the **YEAR** was the "Face with Tears of Joy" emoji.

Japanese researchers built a **HUMANOID ROBOT** that can laugh and smile.

In 1950, an American sound engineer created the **LAUGH TRACK**, a recording of audience laughter, to be used during **COMEDY TV SHOWS** that were recorded without live audiences. It is still used today.

THERE'S A **ROBOT** PROGRAMMED TO PERFORM ORIGINAL STAND-UP COMEDY ROUTINES. IT WILL CHANGE OR REVISE THE **JOKES** IT TELLS BASED ON **AUDIENCE** REACTIONS.

I TOOK A SICK DAY BECAUSE I HAD A VIRUS.

CHAPTER 3

Side-splittingly Spooky

A witch's cat is called a familiar. It's believed that the cat would assist witches in the practice of magic.

KNOCK, KNOCK.

Who's there?

Voodoo.

Voodoo who?

Voodoo you think is knocking at your door?

MOM:
I'm going to tell you a story about a haunted refrigerator.
DAUGHTER:
That sounds chilling!

Q What do you get if you cross a Scottish monster and a German cheese?

A The Loch Ness Muenster.

TONGUE TWISTER!

Say this fast three times:

Sasquatch's squashed watches.

Q What do spirits send home while on vacation?

WISH YOU WERE HERE!

A Ghost-cards.

64

Q Why can't **skeletons** play church **music?**

A Because they don't have organs.

RIDDLE ✹ ME THIS

I don't speak unless **spoken to.** Many have **heard** me but none have **seen me. What am I?**

An echo.

Did you know that there are both **good** and **bad** superstitions around **black cats?**

In Japan, they are believed to bring good luck.

ANYONE KNOW HOW TO START THIS THING?

Q What is a **zombie's** favorite **hairstyle?**

A Deadlocks.

DAD: I don't want to be buried in a cemetery.
SON: Why not?
DAD: I'm not dead yet!

Q Where do **vampires** keep their **Easter eggs?**

A In their Easter caskets.

65

Q How does the Abominable Snowman build his house?

A Igloos it together.

Q How does a skeleton call his friends?

A On the tele-bone.

Q What position does a ghost play on a soccer team?

A Ghoul-keeper.

Q Why does **Dracula annoy his friends?**

A Because he's a pain in the neck.

Q Why won't you find cattle at scary movies?

A Because they are cow-ards.

RIDDLE ☀ ☀ ME THIS

It comes in only one color, but many different sizes. It lives where there's light but will die in the rain. What is it?

Your shadow.

Q What position does the invisible man play on his hockey team?

A No one knows.

Q What kind of shoes does a ghost wear?

A Booooots.

DRACULA: I'd like to write a book about my life.
GHOUL: Maybe you should hire a ghostwriter.
DRACULA: I'm hoping it will be a best seller.
GHOUL: Then you can start a fang club!

66

Some people once believed
that dun-colored (brown or
gray) duck eggs were bad luck.

KNOCK,
KNOCK.

Who's there?
Witches.
Witches who?
Witches the way home?
I think I'm lost.

KNOCK, 💥 KNOCK.

Who's there?

Fangs.

Fangs who?

Fangs for inviting me over.

Q Who do monsters buy cookies from?

A The Ghoul Scouts.

Q What do **witches** use to **style** their **hair?**

A Scare spray.

RIDDLE ✸ ✸ ME THIS

Three men were hunting **Bigfoot** when it started to rain. Only two of them got their hair wet. How is that possible?

The third man was bald.

PATIENT: I think I was bitten by a vampire.
DOCTOR: Take a drink of water.
PATIENT: Will it make me better?
DOCTOR: No, but I'll be able to see if your neck leaks.

Snakes can regrow their fangs quickly when they break or wear out. Some species have up to six fangs developing in their gums at one time.

Q What do **vampires** take for a **sore throat?**

A Coffin drops.

Q Why did the witches' team lose the baseball game?

A Their bats flew away.

Q What has large fangs and says "baa"?

A A ram-pire.

Q What do you call a hot dog bun with nothing inside it?

A A hollow-weenie.

SAY WHAT?

YOU'RE JUST MY TYPE ... O-NEGATIVE!

Bats can eat up to 1,200 mosquitoes in one hour.

I PUT WHIPPED SCREAM ON MY SUNDAES.

I STOPPED IN AT MY FRIEND'S PLACE FOR A BITE OF DINNER. IT WAS FANG-TASTIC!

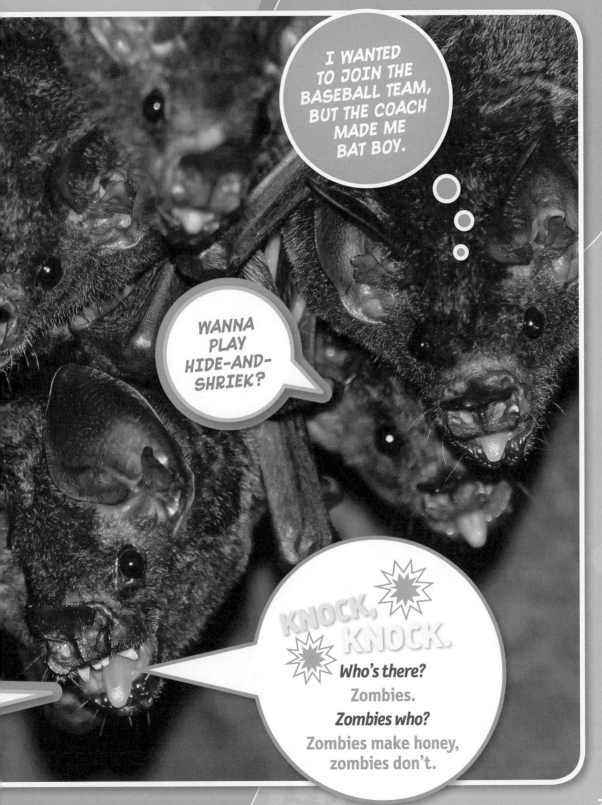

71

R.I.P.

Al B. Bach

AUTHOR:
I think I have writer's block.
EDITOR:
Why don't you head to the cemetery? There's lots of plots there.

R.I.P.

Ricky D. Bones

LAUGHABLE LIST

NOT VERY SCARY MONSTERS:

☐ The Toe Tickler
☐ Abominable Sno-Kone
☐ The Sock-less Monster
☐ Soup-acabra

GHOUL:
Why do you think we get along so well?
DEMON:
Because demons are a ghouls best friend!

CAH! CAH ... OR IS THAT A TRUCK?

Q

What string instrument does a **ghost play?**

Q What time is it when Godzilla sits on your bed?

A Time to get a new bed.

Q What is Bigfoot's favorite month?

WARNING!

PLEASE DO NOT FEED THE SASQUATCH

A Oc-toe-ber.

Did you know that **crows** are **extremely intelligent birds** with amazing problem-solving **skills**?

Researchers have found that crows are able to recognize the faces of humans they have met before.

RIDDLE ME THIS

What runs around a haunted house but doesn't move?

A fence.

Q What did the ghost cook for his dinner party?

A Spook-etti and ghoulash.

A A spook-ulele.

73

DRACULA WAS SITTING AT HOME ONE DAY WHEN THE DOORBELL RANG. When he opened the door, a six-foot (1.8-m)-tall cockroach kicked him in the shins and ran away.

The next evening, there was a knock at the door. When he opened it, there was the same cockroach. Before Dracula could say anything, the cockroach poked him in the eye and ran away.

On the third evening, the cockroach broke into Dracula's house, smashed his TV, knocked over his plants, and hit Dracula on the head. Dracula crawled to the phone and dialed 911. At the hospital, the doctor was very concerned.

"Can you tell me what happened?" the doctor asked. Dracula told him the events of the last three nights.

"Yes, it's not surprising," the doctor said. "There's definitely a nasty bug going around."

A group of foxes
is called a skulk
or a leash.

KNOCK,
KNOCK.

Who's there?

Weirdo.

Weirdo who?

**Weirdo you keep your
Halloween costumes?**

Say this
fast three times:

Haunted houses house *horrifying* haunts.

Q What does Dracula take when he is sick?

A Bite-amins.

Q What do you call a monster with no neck?

A The Lost Neck Monster.

Q Why was the werewolf banned from the butcher shop?

A He was caught chop-lifting.

Q Which is a witch's favorite subject?

A Spelling.

LAUGHABLE LIST

TERRIBLE HALLOWEEN TREATS:

☐ Scabby Taffy—pick your favorite flavor.

☐ Taran-chew-las—bite into them before they bite you.

☐ Pickled Pumpkin Guts— eat till you bust a gut!

☐ Furry Fun Dip—now with 10 percent more hair!

Q What do ghosts bring their dates?

A A boo-quet of flowers.

VAMPIRE 1:
What did you think of that Dracula movie?
VAMPIRE 2:
It was fang-tastic!

SSSHH ... DID YOU HEAR THAT NOISE?

I'M SCARED ... I'M GOING TO SQUEAL.

KNOCK, 💥
💥 KNOCK.
Who's there?
Tyson.
Tyson who?
Tyson garlic around your neck to keep the vampires away.

I DON'T KNOW WHY I LOST MY JOB AT THE PETTING ZOO.

MONSTER 1: What is your son studying at medical school?
MONSTER 2: Nothing, they're studying him!

Q Why did the vampire go to the library?
A He was looking for a book to sink his teeth into.

Orange tabby cats are almost always male.

Q What happened when the werewolf swallowed a clock?
A He got ticks.

GARY: Did you hear that the invisible man married the invisible woman and had a baby?
NICO: Is the baby cute?
GARY: She's nothing to look at.

Q Where does a ghoul water-ski?
A On Lake Eerie.

Q Why do zombies make great employees?

Q What do ghosts use to clean their hair?
A Sham-boo!

Q What is a scarecrow's favorite fruit?
A Straw-berries.

A Because they are dead-icated.

OPTOMETRIST: Your eyesight is terrible.

GHOST: What can I do about it?

OPTOMETRIST: I can fit you with a pair of spook-tacles.

Q What's big and HAIRY and has three wheels?

A A Bigfoot on a tricycle.

RIDDLE ✹ ✹ ME THIS

I dig tiny holes and **fill them** with **silver** or **gold**. I also can build **bridges of silver** and **crowns of gold**. Sooner or later **everyone** sees me, but most are afraid of me. **Who am I?**

The dentist.

Q What do **witches** order at **fancy** hotels?

A Broom service.

Did you know that there is a **species of frog** that will **break its own bones** to create **claws** in order to protect itself?

The end result looks like a cat's claw protruding from the frog's toes.

HE'S RIGHT BEHIND ME, ISN'T HE?

Q What kind of cereal does a yeti eat?

A Snowflakes.

Q What kind of lock does a ghost have on its front door?

A A dead bolt.

Q Who won the skeleton beauty pageant?

A Nobody.

WAITER ON CRUISE SHIP: Would you like to see a menu, sir?

WEREWOLF: No thanks, just bring me the passenger list.

Q What does a **monster** put in its **coffee?**

A Scream and sugar.

SAY WHAT?

NAMES Trick and Treat

FAVORITE ACTIVITY
Shopping at the
ghost-ery store

FAVORITE TOY
Our owner's old
booooooo-ts

PET PEEVE
Laundry day

GHOST DOGS ARE TERRIER-FYING!

In some parts of the world, it was believed that phantom dogs guarded entries to the underworld, and you would die if you looked directly at one.

83

A tiger's roar can be heard from almost two miles (3 km) away.

KNOCK, KNOCK.

Who's there?
Bee.
Bee who?
Bee-ware, there's a full moon tonight.

Q What do you call a **zombie** that is pressing your **doorbell?**

A A dead ringer.

KNOW ANY GOOD DENTISTS?

Q How did the scarecrow fix the hole in his pants?

A With a pumpkin patch.

Q What do you get if you cross a witch with Rice Krispies?

A Snap, cackle, and pop!

WAITER: Welcome to Soul Food, may I take your order?
GHOST: I'll have the boo-logna sandwich.

Q What **quacks** and has **feathers** and **fangs?**

A Count Duckula.

Q What do you call a large Irish spider?

A Paddy longlegs.

Q What's as sharp as a vampire's fang?

A The other fang.

Q What has **one eye, purple** spots, prickles, and **eats rocks?**

A A one-eyed, purple-spotted, prickled, rock-eater.

85

KNOCK,

KNOCK.

Who's there?

Ooze.

Ooze who?

Ooze that monster creeping up on you?!

Green crested lizards are bright green but can turn brown when threatened.

Q What kind of **makeup** do **zombie models** wear?

A Ma-scare-a.

Q What time do man-eating monsters wake up?

A Ate o'clock.

Q Which monster plays the best tricks on his friends?

A Prank-enstein.

Q Which **ghost** is the best **dancer?**

A The boogie man.

Q How does a girl vampire flirt with her boyfriend?

A She bats her eyes.

Q What do you call **two spiders** who just got **married?**

A Newly-webs.

Q What kind of vehicle does Bigfoot drive?

A A monster truck.

KID: Trick or treat!
WOMAN: What are you supposed to be?
KID: A werewolf.
WOMAN: But you aren't wearing a costume.
KID: Well, it isn't a full moon yet.

LOL SPOOKY

A **COMEDY CLUB** in Hollywood, California, U.S.A., is reportedly **haunted** by the **GHOST** of a **COMEDIAN** who was banned from performing there.

Disneyland's **HAUNTED MANSION** ride in California, U.S.A., is reported to have **999 HAPPY HAUNTS** residing in it.

The **DEOGEN** is a **GHOST** said to haunt a forest in Belgium. It appears as a **GREENISH FOG** and sounds like a **child laughing.**

In Brazil it is believed that a **BLACK CAT** walking toward you brings good luck, but if it walks away, it will **TAKE** your good luck with it.

EVERY YEAR, **A PARK IN NEW YORK CITY** HOSTS AN ANNUAL **HALLOWEEN PET PARADE** WHERE HUNDREDS **OF DOGS** IN **COSTUMES** COMPETE IN A **RUNWAY SHOW** TO WIN PRIZES.

ZOLTAR

I SEE TREATS IN YOUR FUTURE.

CHAPTER 4

Absurd Adventures

KNOCK, KNOCK.

Who's there?
Skiis.
Skiis who?
Whose skiis are these?
I found them in
the locker.

The word "ski" comes from
a Norwegian word meaning
"piece of wood."

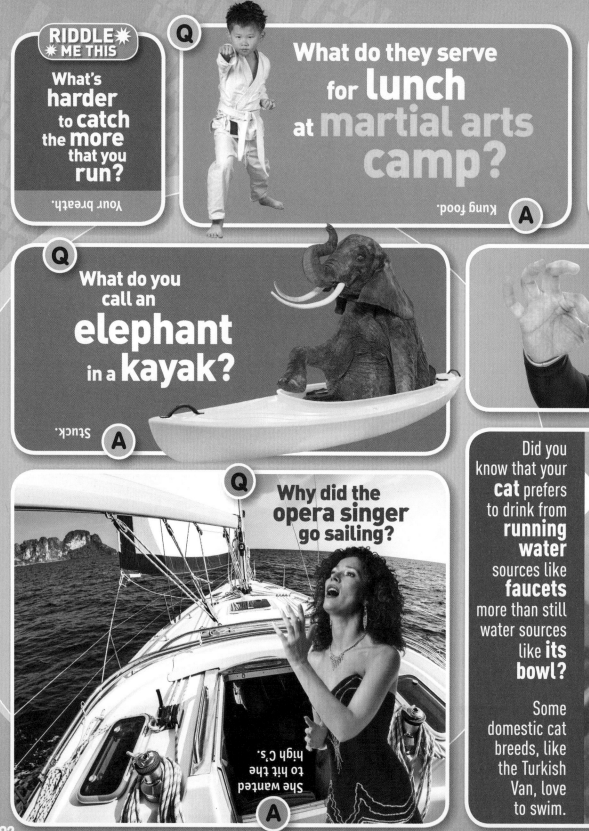

RIDDLE ✳ ✳ ME THIS

What's **harder** to **catch** the **more** that you **run?**

Your breath.

Q What do they serve for **lunch** at **martial arts camp?**

A Kung food.

Q What do you call an **elephant** in a **kayak?**

A Stuck.

Q Why did the **opera singer** go sailing?

A She wanted to hit the high C's.

Did you know that your **cat** prefers to drink from **running water** sources like **faucets** more than still water sources like **its bowl?**

Some domestic cat breeds, like the Turkish Van, love to swim.

92

GINGERBREAD MAN: I hurt my knee while rock climbing today.
GINGERBREAD WOMAN: Have you tried icing it?
GINGERBREAD MAN: Not yet, I've just been using a candy cane.

Q Why are **gymnasts** the best **friends?**

A Because they always bend over backward for people.

Q Why do **scuba divers** fall off the boat **backward** to **enter** the water?

A Because if they fell forward, they'd fall in the boat.

IT'S A PAW-SITIVELY CLAW-SOME DAY FOR SAILING.

Q What do pine trees wear to the lake?

A Swimming trunks.

93

Q What did the cyclist eat when he was in last place?

A Ketchup.

CAMP LEADER: Good morning, campers!
CAMPER: Shhhhh, please don't talk so loud!
CAMP LEADER: Oh! Sorry ... what's wrong?
CAMPER: I've got a sleeping bag, and I don't want to wake it up.

Q Why do puppies make the best kayakers?

A Because they are natural dog paddlers.

BAA, I HERD YOU WERE EASY TO BLEAT.

EWE DON'T STAND A CHANCE AGAINST ME IN THIS RACE.

Q What do you call **four bullfighters** that fall in **quicksand?**

A Quattro sinko.

Q What's the hardest part about skydiving?

A The ground.

Q Why isn't **tanning** a competitive **sport?**

A Because you can only get bronze.

KATE: Are you all ready for our mountain climbing trip?
MICHAELA: Yep, I'm in peak condition!

A leopard kills its prey with one fierce bite to the throat, but it can also deliver a fatal blow to smaller prey with its large paws.

KNOCK, KNOCK.

Who's there?

Woo.

Woo who?

Wow! You are really excited to have visitors!

KNOCK, KNOCK.

Who's there?
Canoe.
Canoe who?
Canoe open this door? I'm tired of knocking.

Q Why did the chicken cross the basketball court?

A Because the ref called a foul.

Q What do you get if you cross a fishing lure and an old gym sock?

A A hook, line, and stinker.

Q What do **archers** wear when they want to get **dressed up?**

A Bow ties.

Q What happens to skydivers when it rains?

A They get wet.

LAUGHABLE ≣LIST≣

CRAZY CAMPSITES:

☐ Camp Soggy Bottom—leakiest tents around!

☐ Camp Eyedont Wannago—voted least popular camp since 2006.

☐ Camp Itchy—we have four types of bedbugs!

☐ Camp Rickety Pines—you don't want to set your tent up under those trees.

A puffin's beak changes color during the year. It's bright orange in the spring and changes to a dull gray in the winter.

JIM: Want to go rock climbing with me?
ELLEN: I would if I was boulder.

RIDDLE ✳ ✳ ME THIS

Two fathers and two sons go fishing, but there are only three people in the boat. How is this possible?

It was a grandfather, a father, and a son on the fishing trip.

WE'RE NATURAL-BORN SNORKELERS!

Q What's big, scary, and carries binoculars?

A A monster on safari.

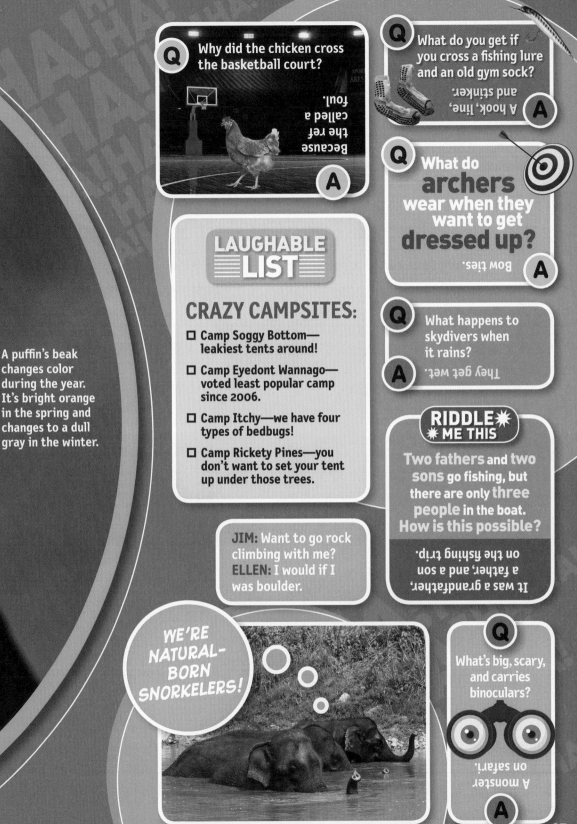

NAME Otto

FAVORITE ACTIVITY
Floating with my
significant otter

FAVORITE FOOD
Seafood

PET PEEVE
Hard-to-catch fish

I OTTER LEAVE FOR MY TRIP NOW.

IS THE RIVER BANK STILL OPEN? I NEED SOME CASH.

I'M GOING TO HAVE AN OTTER-LY GREAT VACATION!

River otters are playful adventure-seekers. They are often spotted diving up to 60 feet (18 m) underwater, belly flopping into rivers, or sliding down muddy hills on their tummies.

Q What do you get if you cross a **musical instrument** and a **snorkeler?**

A A tuba diver.

Q What do you call a girl hanging onto a basketball hoop?

A Annette.

Q Why is **basketball** such a **messy** sport?

A Because you dribble on the floor.

THOSE SKATEBOARDING LESSONS ARE REALLY PAYING OFF!

GUIDE: If you look to your left, you'll see a talking giraffe.
TOURIST: Wow! He's really talking up a storm!
GUIDE: Yes, he's giving a speech on the solar system but it's kind of hard to hear.
TOURIST: Oh well, it's way over my head anyway.

Q Why aren't sumo wrestlers friends with race car drivers?

A Because they move in different circles.

Did you know that many **dogs** have learned to perform human sports like **skate-boarding, surfing,** and **water-skiing?**

Flyball is a dog sport where four pooches work together to complete a relay obstacle course.

RIDDLE ✷ ✷ ME THIS

A man rode into the **Grand Canyon** for a camping tour on **Friday,** stayed for two nights, and **left** on **Friday.** How is this possible?

His mule's name was Friday.

What **activity** does the **sun** enjoy?

Q

Solar-blading.

A

ALLISON: I used to have a fear of hurdles.
DIEGO: How did you get over it?

101

TINA AND LOUISE WERE HIKING ON A SAVANNA WHEN TINA YELLED, "WOW! DID YOU SEE THAT OSTRICH RUN BY?"

"Uh … no, I didn't," Louise said sheepishly.

"What?" Tina says, "It was huge—I can't believe you missed it!"

They hiked on and a few minutes later, Tina exclaimed, "Wow! That was amazing! Did you see that elephant? It just crossed our path on the trail ahead."

Embarrassed, Louise replied, "Oh … no, I didn't see it."

"I can't believe you missed it," Tina says. Thirty seconds later, Tina looked back and at Louise and yelled, "Whoa! Did you see that?"

Louise was annoyed at this point. "Yes, I did!" she lied.

Tina replied, "Then why did you step in it?"

KNOCK, KNOCK.

Who's there?
Adolph.
Adolph who?
Adolph ball hit me in the mouf.

A gorilla's hands and feet are a lot like a human's—they have thumbs and big toes that can grasp and hold on to things.

Q What kind of workouts do chickens follow?

A Egg-cercize routines.

Q What kind of money do fishermen make?

A Net profits.

Q Which highway does a tree take on a road trip?

A Root 66.

Q What do you do if you go on safari and a lion wants to sleep in your tent?

A Sleep somewhere else.

Q Where do monkeys get all their gossip?

A Through the apevine.

RIKU: Are you going to watch the fishing competition today?
KEVIN: Is it online?
RIKU: Yes, but I can't get a good stream.

I WANTED TO GO WHITE WATER RAFTING BUT FORGOT MY RAFT.

Q What's worse than having a snake in your sleeping bag?

A Two snakes in your sleeping bag.

Polar bears are extremely strong swimmers. They can swim continuously for several hours at a time and cover great distances.

KNOCK, KNOCK.

Who's there?

Scold.

Scold who?

Scold enough out here for ice skating.

Q Why did the invisible man turn down a free kayaking trip?

A He just couldn't see himself doing it.

Q How can you tell if the tree you are camping under is a dogwood?

A By the bark.

Q When does the **Golden Gate Bridge** get **angry?**

A When someone crosses it.

FISHERMAN 1: Is this river good for fish?
FISHERMAN 2: It must be, I can't get any of them to leave!

Q Why did the **kayaker** cross the **Atlantic?**

A To get to the other tide.

Q Why did the cookie go to the doctor after hiking?

A Because it was feeling crumby.

Q Which **race** is never **run?**

A A swimming race.

Q How did the lobster take a tour of the Grand Canyon?

A By shell-icopter.

SKIER 1: I can't find my sister; she was just near the chairlift.
SKIER 2: She's gondola top of the mountain.

Q How do **fleas** travel?

A They go itch-hiking.

Q What do you call a **playlist** on a **hiker's** music player?

A A trail mix.

SURE, I ENJOYED THE CLIMB UP, BUT HOW DO WE GET DOWN?

Q Where does a **cruise ship** go when it's not feeling well?

A To the dock-tor.

RIDDLE ME THIS

A baseball team won 5-0 but not a single man ran around the bases. How is that possible?

All the men were married.

108

SURFER 1: Hey, why are you wearing a baseball mitt?
SURFER 2: Because you said we were going to catch some waves.

Did you know that within **one day** of being **born,** a baby **mountain goat,** or kid, can climb rocks and mountains with its mother?

You can tell the age of a mountain goat by counting the rings on its horns.

Q What do you get if you cross a creek and a river?

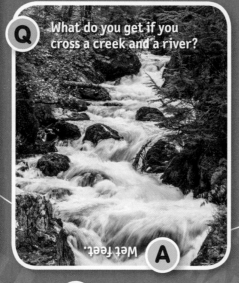

Wet feet. **A**

Q

What do
chickens do on
Sunday afternoons?

They go on peck-nics. **A**

109

SAY WHAT?

WADDLE WE DO TODAY?

NAMES
Slipper and Slider

FAVORITE ACTIVITY
Skiing

FAVORITE FOOD
Snow cones

PET PEEVE
Wearing the same outfit as someone else

I LOVE CHILLIN' WITH MY PEEPS.

While penguins are molting, or shedding their feathers, they can't go in the water to hunt. They have to fatten themselves up to prepare for fasting during these few weeks.

IF WE GO CROSS-COUNTRY SKIING, CAN WE AT LEAST START WITH A SMALL COUNTRY?
KNOCK, KNOCK.
Who's there?
Snow.
Snow who?
Snow time to lose! Let's get moving!
LET'S JUST PLAY IT COOL.

The puma goes by many names: panther, mountain lion, and catamount.

KNOCK, KNOCK.

Who's there?
Tennis.
Tennis who?
Tennis five plus five.

RIDDLE ✹ ME THIS

At what **school** do you have to **drop out** in order to **graduate?**

Skydiving school.

Q Why aren't artists good at sports?

A Every game ends in a draw.

Q Why shouldn't you play **football** with a **pig?**

A Because he'll hog the ball.

Q Why did the teacher wear sunglasses on her school trip?

A Because her students were so bright.

Q What **lights up** a stadium?

A A soccer match.

CUSTOMER: I'm leaving for my cruise, and I need to pick up my laundry.
DRY CLEANER: Okay, let me just see if I can find it.
CUSTOMER: Hurry! Hurry! I don't want to miss my boat.
DRY CLEANER: All right, all right, keep your shirt on.

Q What did the **sardine** call the **submarine tour?**

A A can of people.

Q How did the **barber** win the **cross-country race?**

A He took a shortcut.

Q Which baseball player pours the lemonade?

A The pitcher.

113

KNOCK, ✸
✸ **KNOCK.**

Who's there?
Safari.
Safari who?
Safari so good.

Q Which **people travel** the most?

A Roam-ans.

MARATHON RUNNER: I'm here for my pre-race checkup, doc.
DOCTOR: Well, you seem to be in fantastic condition. Your pulse is like clockwork.
MARATHON RUNNER: That's because your finger is on my watch!

Q What do **birds** use when **skydiving?**

A Sparrow-chutes.

Q Why did the orange stop climbing halfway up the mountain?

A It ran out of juice.

Q What do you call the **slowest competitor** in a downhill **ski race?**

A A slope-poke.

Q Which is the **noisiest sport?**

A Racket-ball.

An elephant's ears release body heat to help keep it cool in hot temperatures.

Q Why **didn't** the **girl take** the **bus home** from her **camping trip?**

A Because her mom would make her bring it back.

Q What does the **winner** of a **marathon lose?**

A Her breath.

CARRIE: I'm learning to surf in my kitchen.
CHARLOTTE: Where?
CARRIE: On a micro-wave!

LOL ADVENTURE

In 2015, a woman set a **WORLD RECORD** for fastest marathon run while dressed as a **FAST-FOOD ITEM.**

Despite their funny appearance, **RODEO CLOWNS** are trained bullfighters whose primary job is protecting fallen riders from the **BULLS.**

Runners in an annual Seattle, U.S.A., **marathon** can **EAT CAKE** at aid stations and rest on **COUCHES** along the **running** course.

In the 1800s, **WATER POLO** was played on floating barrels that looked like **HORSES.**

OUTHOUSES ARE PLACED ON SKIS AND PUSHED TO THE FINISH LINE AT THE OUTHOUSE RACES IN TRENARY, MICHIGAN, U.S.A.

CHAPTER 5

Wacky World

KNOCK, KNOCK.

Who's there?

Japan.

Japan who?

Japan on the stove is hot, don't pick it up.

A woman and her dog traveled the world for eight months to raise awareness for dog adoption. They visited dog shelters on five continents during their trip.

PASSPORT

119

GARRY:
What channel are the Japanese origami championships on?
ROBERTO:
You can only watch it on paper-view.

Q Where do Canadian sheep come from?

A Manito-baa.

HAS ANYONE SEEN MY MUMMY?

Q What kind of pastry comes from Britain?

A An English muffin.

TONGUE TWISTER!

Say this fast three times:

Norwegian boys need noisy, annoying toys.

DINER:
Oh no! My Hawaiian pizza is burnt!

WAITER:
Sorry, we should have cooked it at aloha temperature.

Did you know that the **Pyramid** of **Khufu** at **Giza** is the largest **Egyptian pyramid?**

It's estimated to be made up of about 2.4 million stone blocks weighing 2.5 tons (2.3 t) each.

RIDDLE ME THIS

What travels **around** the **world,** but **never leaves** its **corner?**

A stamp.

Q

What can you find in the **middle** of the **ocean?**

The letter e.

A

Q

What do **Canadians** **score** on their **tests?**

Ehs.

A

Q Which country has the most birds?

A Portu-gull.

Q Which city receives the most deliveries?

A Parcel-ona.

JOSH: Where do you want to go on vacation?
DYLAN: I'd like to go to Holland, wooden shoe?

Q Why don't seals go on vacation in the United Kingdom?

A Because they're afraid of Wales.

Q What keeps lions from leaving the savanna?

A The ele-fence.

Q What did Tennessee?

A The same thing Arkansas.

Q What do you call a rabbit in a kilt?

A Hop Scotch.

THE WORST PART ABOUT TRAVEL IS PACKING.

122

KNOCK, KNOCK.

Who's there?

Iraq.

Iraq who?

Iraq-ed my brain to think of something fun to do.

Churchill, in Manitoba, Canada, is the polar bear capital of the world. The bears pass through the city during their migration.

KNOCK, KNOCK.

Who's there?
Iran.
Iran who?
Iran all the
way here.

Blue eyes are common in just a
few dog breeds, such as Siberian
huskies and Australian shepherds.

Q Where do angry chickens come from?

A Mad-egg-ascar.

Q What's the **craziest** way **to travel?**

A By loco-motive.

Q Why does the Mississippi River see so well?

A Because it has four i's.

Q What is the Amazon rain forest's favorite month?

A Sep-timber.

Q Where in the United States do you find the funkiest dancers?

A San Fran-disco.

JULIA: Jamaica dinner yet? I'm hungry.
EWAN: Not yet, but Alaska everyone what they want to eat.

TONGUE 🌀 **TWISTER!**

Say this fast three times:

The **gracious Greek geek agreed.**

I KNEW WE SHOULD HAVE GOTTEN HERE EARLY. TOURISTS FLOCK TO THIS PLACE.

Q Which **country eats** the **most soup?**

A Bowl-ivia.

125

SAY WHAT?

NAMES Latitude and Longitude

FAVORITE ACTIVITY Leisurely Sunday drives

FAVORITE TOY GPS

PET PEEVE Speeding tickets

I HAVE A FEAR OF SPEED BUMPS, BUT I'M SLOWLY GETTING OVER IT.

WE'RE GOING ON A THREE-WEEK VACATION ... WE'RE GOING TO WALK TO THE OTHER SIDE OF THIS FOREST.

THIS VACATION IS GOING TO BE SLOTHSOME!

I LOVE TRAVELING SLOW MUCH!

Sloths live in tropical climates in Central and South America.

126

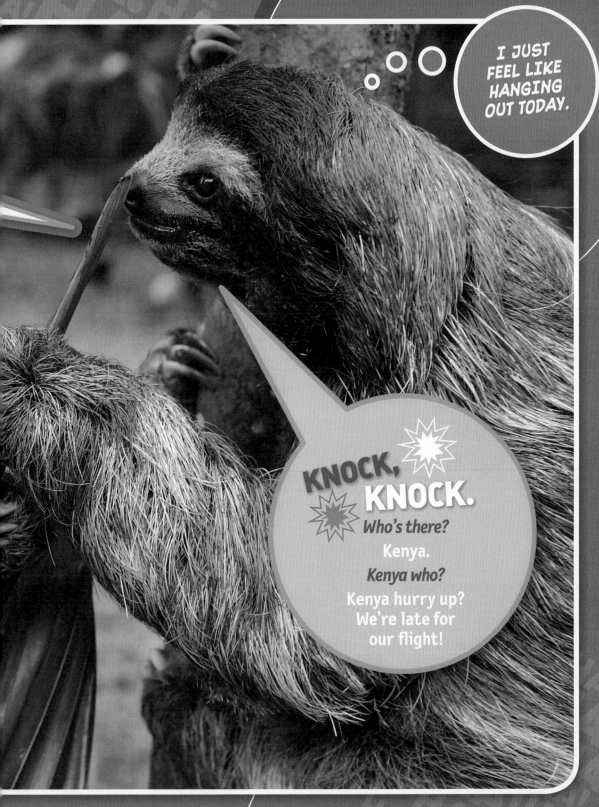

I JUST FEEL LIKE HANGING OUT TODAY.

KNOCK, KNOCK.

Who's there?

Kenya.

Kenya who?

Kenya hurry up? We're late for our flight!

127

Q

Which country has the most marathons?

A Iran.

TEACHER: Why didn't you study for your geography test?

ASTRONAUT: My dad says the world is changing every day so I thought I'd wait until it stops.

LAUGHABLE LIST

SIGNS YOU ARE DRIVING THROUGH A DESERT ON YOUR ROAD TRIP:

- ☐ You eat hot wings to cool your mouth off.
- ☐ When the temperature drops below 98°F (37°C), you put on a sweater.
- ☐ Cows are giving evaporated milk.
- ☐ The cacti are sitting in the shade.
- ☐ Vultures are taking the day off.

ANTHONY: Where were you born?
PRIYA: In India.
ANTHONY: Which part?
PRIYA: All of me!

Did you know that **Machu Picchu's** construction is still a **mystery?**

It's not known how the massive stone blocks were moved up the steep terrain and through thick jungles.

Q Which state is the loudest?

A Illi-noise.

RIDDLE ✹ ME THIS

At **night** they come without being called. In the **morning** they are **lost** without being stolen. **What are they?**

Stars.

Q Why is the **River Thames** so rich?

A Because it has two banks.

MACHU PICCHU PHOTOBOMB!

Q Which country never stays still?

A Romania.

129

A MOTHER WAS WALKING BY HER DAUGHTER'S ROOM one night and saw her daughter staring out the window. "What are you doing, sweetie?" the mother asked.

"I'm making a wish on that shooting star," the girl replied.

"Oh, that's nice. What are you wishing for?" her mother asked.

"I'm wishing that the capital of the United States is Albany," the girl answered.

Her mother looked confused and said, "Why would you wish for something so strange?"

The daughter replied, "Because that's what I wrote on my geography test."

Some goats will climb trees in order to eat the hanging fruit.

KNOCK, KNOCK.

Who's there?

Atlas.

Atlas who?

Atlas I've returned from my trip around the world!

Helga is hoping to hop to Tahiti.

Q Which U.S. city has the most chickens?

A Chick-ago.

Q What did the Kinderdijk windmills say to the visiting movie star?

A "I'm your biggest fan!"

Q Which is the **spiciest country?**

A Chile.

Q Who is a penguin's favorite relative?

A Aunt Arctica.

Q What type of planes do snakes travel on?

A Boeing constrictors.

Q Why should you **never** play hide-and-seek with **Mount Everest?**

A Because it always peaks.

Q Why did the **Louvre pyramid** go to the **doctor?**

A Because it had window panes.

TEACHER: Where is the English Channel?
MARY: It must be far away because my TV doesn't pick it up.

A group of tortoises
is called a creep.

KNOCK,
KNOCK.
Who's there?
Juneau.
Juneau who?
Juneau how cold
Alaska is?

Q What is **Mount Rushmore's** favorite **music?**

A Rock-and-roll.

Q Which **state has terrible allergies?**

A Mass-achoo-setts.

Q What is Mount Etna's favorite meal?

A Magma-roni and cheese.

Q How do you open the **Great Lakes?**

A With the Florida Keys.

SON: Where do bees come from?
MOTHER: Sting-apore and Bee-livia.

Q Where do you find an **ocean** without **water?**

A On a map.

Q Where do you take your **unpaid electric bill?**

A I-owe-a.

Q What do you call an Australian boomerang that doesn't come back after you throw it?

A A stick.

Q Which **state** has the **cleanest clothes?**

A Wash-ington.

Q How do Notre-Dame Cathedral's statues cure their sore throats?

A By gargoyling.

TEACHER: Can anyone tell me where elephants are found?

STUDENT: How does anyone lose an elephant?!

Q Why doesn't anyone want to be **friends** with **Big Ben?**

A Because all it does it tock, tock, tock.

I'M SURE THE EIFFEL TOWER IS AROUND HERE SOMEWHERE! I WISH I HAD A MAP.

Q Why can't you **trust the Atlantic Ocean?**

A Because there is something fishy about it.

136

Did you know that some **pigeons** were **war heroes?** Messenger pigeons carried notes and intelligence from behind enemy lines during **World War I** and **World War II.**

Pigeons can be found on every continent except Antarctica.

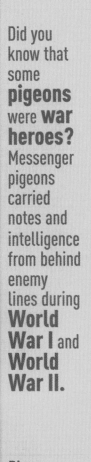

TRAVELER 1: How was your trip?
TRAVELER 2: Great! I got Hungary in Italy, so I ate some Turkey. How was your trip?
TRAVELER 1: Not so good, I slipped on Greece and got bitten by Wales.

Q How did Christopher Columbus's men **sleep** on their **ships?**

A With their eyes closed.

Q Why can't you make a **reservation** at the **Library** of **Congress?**

A Because it's completely booked.

Q What state has the most horses?

A Neigh-braska.

SAY WHAT?

NAME
Globe Trotter

FAVORITE ACTIVITY
Horsing around

FAVORITE DANCE
The Neigh Neigh

PET PEEVE
Bad weather ...
especially reins

QUIT STALLING, IT'S TIME TO LEAVE!

KNOCK, KNOCK.

Who's there?
Neigh.
Neigh who?
I just met your neighbors.

WE DON'T WANT TO MISS THE MANE EVENT.

Horses sleep standing up. They "lock" their legs to stop themselves from collapsing while asleep.

138

A baby goose, or gosling, can dive and swim up to 30 feet (9 m) underwater when it is a day old.

KNOCK, KNOCK.

Who's there?
Europe.
Europe who?
Europe to no good!

RIDDLE ✸ ME THIS

They **run fast** but can't stand. You **ride them** like **horses** but they don't eat grass. You can **find** them all over the world. What are they?

Bicycles.

LOCKSMITH 1: Where do you want to go on vacation?
LOCKSMITH 2: To the Florida Keys.

Q What do you get if you cross **Godzilla** and a **kangaroo**?
A Great big holes all over Australia.

Q **What kind of hair does the Atlantic Ocean have?**
A Wavy.

Q What is the cheapest way to travel?
A By sale-boat.

Q Why did the sailors carry a bar of soap with them?
A In case they got shipwrecked, they could wash themselves up on shore.

SOAP

Q Where do fish keep their money?
A In the riverbank.

OH BOY, WE DEFINITELY OVERPACKED.

IAN: Can a bunny hop higher than the Empire State Building?
BEN: Yes, the Empire State Building can't hop.

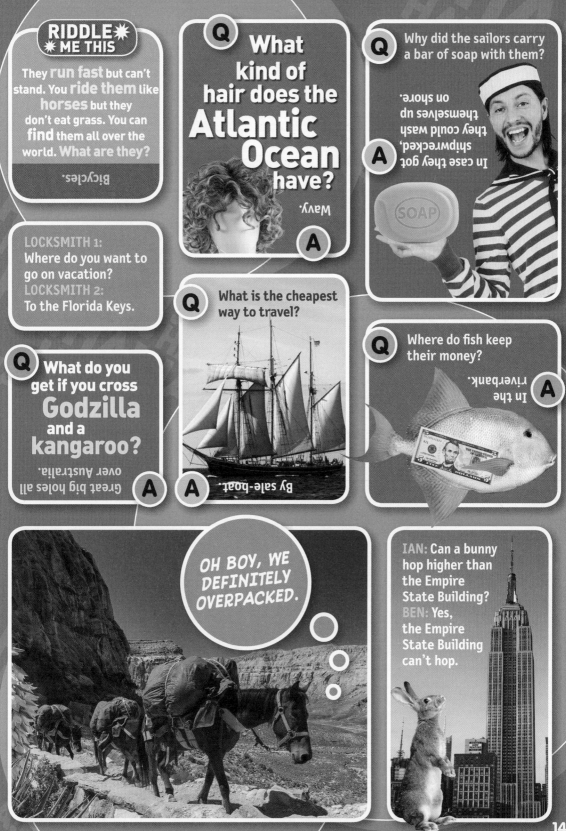

Koalas rarely drink water. They get most of the moisture they need from eating eucalyptus leaves.

KNOCK, KNOCK.

Who's there?
Havana.
Havana who?
Havana great time in Cuba!

Q Which landmark has the best manners?

A The Leaning Tower of Please-a.

Q What do you call a type of Mexican food served at the North Pole?

A Brrr-itos.

Q Which little rivers run into the Nile?

A Juve-niles.

Q Which rock group has four men that don't sing?

A Mount Rushmore.

Q What is the capital of France?

A The letter F.

Q What do you get if you cross a farm animal and a mapmaker?

A A cow-tographer.

Q Which state is the hardest to find?

A Dela-where?

Q Why was the vacationing doctor so angry?

A He had no patients.

TEACHER: Jack, point to where America is on the map.
JACK: Right there.
TEACHER: That's correct. Nina, who discovered America?
NINA: Jack did.

LOL WORLD

The first annual **Laughing Championships** were held in Quebec, Canada, in 2001. Contests included: **Best Maniacal Laugh** and **Most Contagious Belly Laugh.**

In **Japan,** it's considered **impolite** to **SHOW YOUR TEETH** while laughing.

A laughter epidemic broke out in a **girls' school** and spread to **1,000 PEOPLE** in Tanzania, Africa, in 1962.

In **Thailand,** people text **"5555"** instead of **"hahaha"** to respond to something **funny.**

MY OPTOMETRIST USES AN EYE-PHONE.

5555

IN SOME PARTS OF SOUTH AFRICA, PEOPLE **THROW FURNITURE OUT THE WINDOW** TO CELEBRATE **NEW YEAR'S DAY.**

HAPPY NEW YEAR

HEY! I LIKED THAT CHAIR!

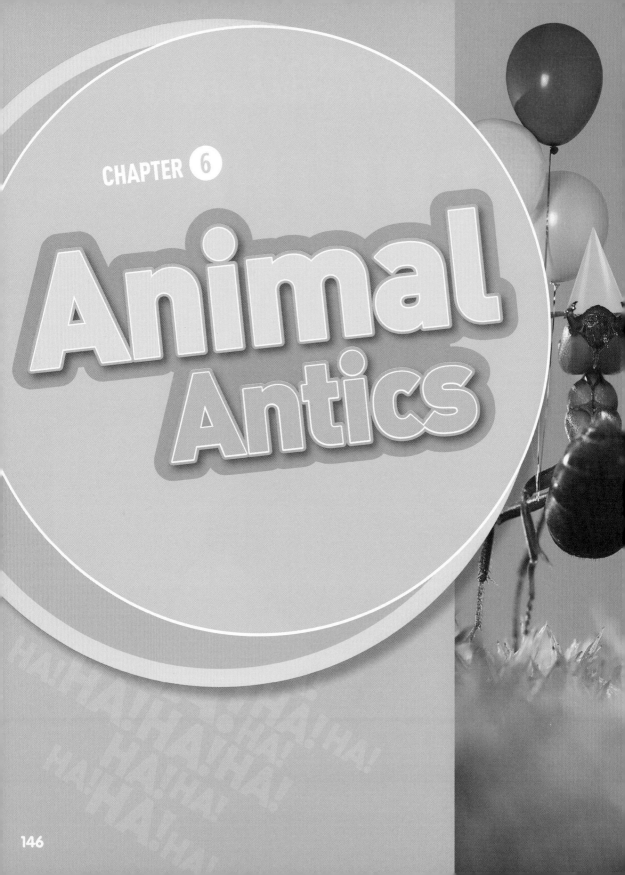

CHAPTER 6

Animal Antics

KNOCK, KNOCK.

Who's there?

Herd.

Herd who?

Herd you were home, want to come out and play?

Ants can carry 50 times their own body weight. That would be like you lifting a car!

LAUGHABLE LIST

NEW DOG BREEDS:

☐ Collie + Lhasa apso = Collapso: folds up to fit into small doghouses

☐ German shepherd + cocker spaniel = Shocker: a dog that's always surprising you

☐ Collie + malamute = Comute: you have to travel a long way to find one

☐ Afghan + Labrador retriever = Afghan retriever: brings you a blanket

☐ Shar-pei + German pointer = Sharp point: be careful when petting this one

SANJIDA: Oh no! 500 hares have escaped from the zoo!
PRIYA: Don't worry, the police are combing the area.
SANJIDA: I hope every bunny gets home safe.

RIDDLE ✷ ME THIS

What grows **up** while growing **down?**

A goose.

I FIND THESE JOKES A-MOOSE-ING!

Q Why did the **pig** drop out of the marathon?

Because it pulled a hamstring. **A**

8725 MARATHO

Q What do you call a member of the weasel family that likes to knit?

A A wool-ver-ine.

Q What do you call **baby owls** that get **stuck** in the rain?

A Moist owlets.

Did you know that a **moose's antlers** can grow to be **six feet (1.8 m) wide** and weigh up to 70 pounds (32 kg)?

Adult moose shed their antlers every winter.

TONGUE TWISTER!

Say this fast three times:

Three-toed tree toad.

Q Why was the **sheep** itchy?

A It had fleece.

COW 1: Hey, who's the new calf?
COW 2: I don't know, I've never seen herbivore.

What do you call a COW that doesn't give milk?

A An udder failure.

What sits when it stands, and jumps when it walks?

A A kangaroo.

Say this fast three times:

A skunk thunk the stump stunk.

Q **Where do lambs share their videos?**

A On ewe-tube.

Q **Why are there different blood types?**

A So mosquitoes can enjoy different flavors.

Q **What do you get if you cross a flower and a zoo animal?**

A A rhinoce-rose.

Q **What do you get if you cross a snake and a piece of fruit?**

A A banana-conda.

Q **Why do cows wear bells around their neck?**

A Because their horns don't work.

ZOO KEEPER 1: Why did you measure this snake in inches?
ZOO KEEPER 2: Because they don't have feet.

The ring-tailed coati is closely related to the raccoon family. It uses its flexible snout to search under rocks and leaves for food.

KNOCK, KNOCK.

Who's there?

Amos.

Amos who?

Amos-quito landed on my nose!

Gulls are able to drink saltwater. They have "salt glands" that filter the salt and trickle the excess out through their nostrils.

KNOCK, KNOCK.

Who's there?
Quack.
Quack who?
Quack another bad joke and I'm leaving.

Q Why did the chicken go to the movies?

A For hen-tertainment.

Q What is a marsupial's favorite soft drink?

A Coca-Koala.

MOM COW: It's time for bed!
CALF: Do I calf to go?
MOM COW: Yes, it's pasture bedtime.

RIDDLE ✹ ME THIS

A **horse** is tied to a 10-foot (3-m) **rope** and there is a bale of hay **20 feet** (6 m) away from him but the horse can still eat from it. **How is that possible?**

The other end of the rope isn't tied to anything.

Q Why did the pig give his girlfriend a box of chocolates?

A Because it was Valen-swine's Day.

Q Why do snails need their shells to race?

A Without them, they are sluggish.

Q What does a penguin eat at a barbecue?

A An iceberg-er.

KEEP LOOKING, I KNOW WE PARKED THE CAR AROUND HERE SOMEWHERE.

153

SAY WHAT?

NAME Barcode

FAVORITE ACTIVITY
Blending in

FAVORITE FOOD
Oreo cookies

PET PEEVE
Lions hogging the
water hole

WHAT'S BLACK AND WHITE AND RED ALL OVER? A ZEBRA WITH A SUNBURN.

I'VE GOT A GREAT APPETITE. I EAT LIKE A HORSE.

A ZEBRA IS A HORSE BEHIND BARS.

WHY CAN'T ZEBRAS PARALLEL PARK? BECAUSE WE DON'T WANT TO STAY BETWEEN THE LIONS.

SPOTS ARE SO LAST SEASON.

A zebra's teeth will grow for its entire life. Zebras graze and chew on tough grasses constantly, which wears their teeth down.

KNOCK, KNOCK.

Who's there?

Rhino.

Rhino who?

Rhino every knock-knock joke there is.

Q Where do **frozen chickens** live?

A In egg-loos.

Q What do you call an owl that does magic tricks?

A Hoo-dini.

EXCUSE ME, SIR ... PARDON ME, MA'AM ... JUST TRYING TO REACH MY SEAT ON THE END.

YOUR FOOT IS IN MY EYE!

Q What do you call a **sneaky pig?**

A Cunningham.

Q What sort of shoes do frogs wear to the beach?

A Open-toad sandals.

Did you know that **tree frogs** have **disc-shaped toes** that give its feet more suction and a better grip?

They live in forests and jungles in warm regions around the world.

RIDDLE ME THIS

If a **rooster** laid a **brown egg** and a **white egg,** what color **chicks** would hatch?

None, roosters don't lay eggs.

NICO: Oh no! My seahorse ran away!
MACEO: Actually, it was more of a scallop.

SQUIRREL 1: You walnut guess what happened! I forget where I buried the cashews!
SQUIRREL 2: You're nuttin' but trouble.

A WOMAN WAS DRIVING AND SAW
A TRUCK BROKEN DOWN ON THE SIDE OF THE
ROAD. The woman pulled over and offered
some help to the driver.

The truck driver said, "That would be great! Can
you please take the 10 lions I have in the back of
my truck to the zoo
while I fix my tire?
I'll give you $50."

The woman agreed. She took the money and the lions and drove away.

Two hours later, the truck driver spotted the woman and the lions walking out of a theater. He pulled over and yelled, "What are you doing? You were supposed to take those lions to the zoo!"

The woman answered, "I did, but **we had some money left over** so we went to the movies!"

KNOCK,
KNOCK.
Who's there?
Herring.
Herring who?
**Herring some awful
knock-knock jokes.**

Lionfish have up to 18
venomous spines which are
used only for self-defense.

Q Why do elephants have trunks?

A Because they don't have pockets to put their stuff in.

Q Where do cows go for lunch?

A The calf-eteria.

FARMER 1: Why does this chicken coop only have two doors?
FARMER 2: Because if it had four it would be a sedan.

Q Why did the farmer cross the road?

A To get his chicken back.

Q Where does a **bull** keep his **important papers?**

A In his beef-case.

Q Where do goats get their medicine?

A From the farm-acy.

Q What do you call an **angry grizzly bear?**

A Furry-ous.

OUR SELFIE GAME IS ON POINT.

161

KNOCK, KNOCK.

Who's there?

Fleas.

Fleas who?

Fleas a jolly good fellow.

I'M JUST GOING TO HAVE A QUICK SNACK, AND THEN IT'S OFF TO SCHOOL.

When confronted by a predator, meerkats will group together, arch their backs, and hiss to try to trick the attacker into thinking they are one large, fierce animal.

RIDDLE ME THIS

Which is heavier, a pound of **chicken feathers** or a **pound of bricks?**

Neither, they both weigh a pound.

Q What do you get if you cross a **shark** and a **cow?**

I don't know, but I wouldn't try to milk it! **A**

Q What do you call a **lazy marsupial?**

Q What do you call a **gossipy monkey?**

A blab-oon. **A**

A pouch potato. **A**

Which **birds** always stick together? **Q**

Vel-crows. **A**

Q What do you get if you cross an elephant and a skin doctor?

A pachyderm-atologist. **A**

BABY CAMEL: Dad, can I have another glass of water?
FATHER CAMEL: Another one? That's the second glass this month!

Q What do you call **two squids** that look **exactly** alike?

Q Which **animal complains the most?**

A A whine-oceros.

BEER... BEAR: I'll have a hamburger and ... fries.
WAITER: Okay, but why the big pause?
BEAR: I was born with them!

LOOK! NO CAVITIES!

Q What do you get if you squeeze an alpaca and a citrus fruit at the same time?

A Llama-nade.

Q How do **grizzlies** keep their dens **cool** in the summer?

A With bear-conditioning.

A I-tentacle twins.

Did you know that the **closest relatives** to the **hippo** are **cetaceans** such as whales and dolphins?

A hippo's ears and nostrils fold shut to keep water out while swimming.

Q

What do **mallards** like to watch on **TV?**

A Duck-umentaries.

Q What **prizes** are awarded at the **pig** Olympics?

A Pork medallions.

Q What do chimpanzees wear when they barbecue?

A Ape-rons.

FELIX: Why does your mother keep saying "Cluck, cluck, cluck"?
STEVE: She thinks she's a chicken.
FELIX: So why don't you stop her?
STEVE: Because we ran out of eggs.

SAY WHAT?

NAME Buck

FAVORITE ACTIVITY
Writing in my journal.
"Deer Diary ..."

FAVORITE FOOD
Cookie doe

PET PEEVE
People who horn in on conversations

I WONDER HOW MUCH A SALT LICK COSTS ... ABOUT A BUCK?

FOR REAL DOE, WHERE CAN I BUY ONE?

I HAVE NO I-DEER.

I'M QUITE FAWNED OF YOU.

DO YOU WANT TO PLAY TRUTH OR DEER?

Antlers are made of bone and can grow up to one inch (2.5 cm) per day.

KNOCK,
KNOCK.

Who's there?

Honeybee.

Honeybee who?

**Honeybee a dear
and grab these
shopping bags.**

While inside the
hive, honeybee
workers will clean
and circulate the
air by beating
their wings.

Q What do you call a group of pigs running toward you?

A A ham-pede.

Q What do cats use to mix pancake batter?

A Their own whiskers.

Q What do you call a thieving alligator?

A A crook-odile.

SHOPPER:
I'd like 30 bags of birdseed, please.
PET STORE OWNER:
Wow! How many birds do you have?
SHOPPER:
None, I'd like to grow some.

Q What side of a cheetah has the most spots?

A The outside.

Q Why did the **pig** stop **sunbathing?**

A Because he was bacon in the heat.

Q What kind of **coffee** do **cows** drink?

Bessie

A De-calf-inated.

Q Why can't an emu fly?

A Because it can't book a flight.

Q What time do **ducks** get out of bed?

A At the quack of dawn.

KNOCK, KNOCK.

Who's there?
Gorilla.
Gorilla who?
I'd love a gorilla cheese sandwich.

Though a mandrill's teeth can look scary, baring them is a friendly gesture among other mandrills.

Q What kind of big cats join you for breakfast?

A Sausage lynx.

Q What do you call a cranky bee?

A A grumble-bee.

LIBRARIAN: Can I help you find anything?
OWL: Can you point me to the mystery section? I love to read hoot-dunits.

Q Which sea creatures hang out at the gym?

A Mussels.

Q What kind of key opens a banana?

A A monkey.

Q Why didn't anyone speak to the pig at the costume party?

A Because everyone thought it was a boar.

Q What kind of fruit do gorillas eat?

A Ape-ricots.

Q Why do centipedes have 100 legs?

A So they can walk.

Q What do you call a penguin in the jungle?

A Lost.

DUCK: Hello, I'd like to buy some lipstick.
SALESPERSON: Sure thing, are you paying with cash or should I put it on your bill?

LOL ANIMALS

Mosquitoes prefer to BITE people with SMELLY feet.

COCKROACHES get gassy from eating cucumbers.

One species of turtle can breathe through its REAR END.

One species of CICADA makes a sound similar to human LAUGHTER.

SPOTTED HYENAS
ARE OFTEN CALLED
LAUGHING HYENAS
BECAUSE OF THE LOUD,
HIGH-PITCHED
GIGGLING SOUND
THEY MAKE.

I'VE GOT A SERIOUS CASE OF THE GIGGLES!

THESE JOKES ARE SO CORN-Y!

KNOCK, KNOCK.

Who's there?
Fairy.
Fairy who?
Fairy tired from my long flight.

The explorer Marco Polo reported seeing unicorns on his travels. He had actually seen a rhinoceros.

TONGUE TWISTER!

Say this fast three times:

A frugal ruler's rural mural.

Q What do you get if you cross a **fairy tale** and a **ghost story?**

A Ghoul-dilocks and the Three Bears.

BRAD:
Did you see the guy at the costume party dressed as half man, half horse?
GABRIEL:
Yes, he certainly was the centaur of attention.

Did you know that the **unicorn** is **Scotland's national animal?**

The unicorn appears in chains on the country's coat of arms to suggest that Scottish kings were strong enough to tame the unicorn.

WHAT DO I WEAR TO WORK? MY UNI-FORM OF COURSE!

RIDDLE ME THIS

What has **six legs, four ears,** and a **suit of armor?**

A prince on horseback.

Q Why do you **never** see **dragons** out during the day?

Because they usually hunt knights.

A

176

Q What's the difference between a goblin and a head of lettuce?

A One is a funny beast and the other is a bunny feast.

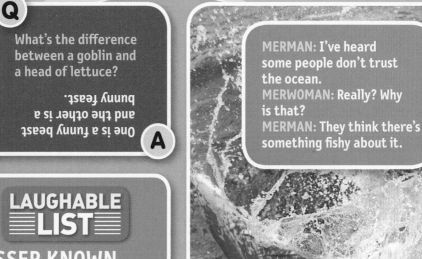

MERMAN: I've heard some people don't trust the ocean.
MERWOMAN: Really? Why is that?
MERMAN: They think there's something fishy about it.

LAUGHABLE LIST

LESSER KNOWN GREEK GODS:

- ☐ Typos—god of proofreaders
- ☐ Mintees—god of fresh breath
- ☐ Spectaclees—god of improved eyesight
- ☐ Cheapos—god of saving money
- ☐ Tartemis—god of tasty pastries
- ☐ Lieclops—god of mistruths

Q What does a Greek goddess do to pamper herself?

A She makes a Hera-pointment.

177

Q Why did Captain Hook cross the road?

A To get to the second-hand shop.

Q What was it like planning **Goliath's funeral?**

A A giant undertaking.

Q Why was **Zeus** so **angry?**

A Someone stole his thunder.

Q What did **Kraken** eat for **lunch?**

A Fish and ships.

Q What do you call someone with a callus on one foot?

A A uni-corn.

MARIE:
Do you know what's in Aladdin's lamp?
MARCUS:
It wouldn't take a genie-ous to find out.

WHO'S THE FAIREST OF THEM ALL?

Q What do you get when you cross an archer and a gift-wrapper?

A Ribbon Hood.

A female brown bear gives birth while hibernating. She won't meet her cubs until she wakes up!

KNOCK, KNOCK.

Who's there?
Hansel.
Hansel who?
Hansel cold, can I borrow some gloves?

Hippos mainly eat at night and can consume up to 150 pounds (68 kg) of grass.

KNOCK, KNOCK.

Who's there?
Gretel.
Gretel who?
We Gretel long great with each other!

Q What do you call the story of "The Three Little Pigs"?

A A pigtail.

Q Why would **Snow White** make a great judge?

A Because she's the fairest in the land.

Q Why did Cinderella get kicked off the baseball team?

A She kept running away from the ball.

Q What do dragons put in their soup?

A Firecrackers.

Q What do you call a fairy that hasn't bathed?

A Stinker-bell.

HUMPTY DUMPTY: Why are all the king's men so short?
KING: They're all 12 inches tall.
HUMPTY DUMPTY: Does that mean they're foot soldiers?

RIDDLE ☀ ME THIS

A **fairy** lives in a **one-story house** with a **blue** couch, **blue** walls, and **blue** carpets. **What color are her stairs?**

There are no stairs in a one-story house.

THIS DOESN'T SEEM AS REGAL AS THE CROWN I HAD WHEN I WAS A HUMAN PRINCE.

Q Why was Cinderella so bad at sports?

A Because she had a pumpkin for a coach.

SAY WHAT?

NAME Thor

FAVORITE ACTIVITY
Home renovations

FAVORITE TOY
Enchanted hammer

PET PEEVE
Hitting my thumb

ODIN SENT SECRET MESSAGES BY NORSE CODE.

I'M A-FREYA-D OF SCARY MYTHS.

A hammerhead shark's head is the perfect shape for trapping stingrays and pinning them to the seafloor before eating them.

KNOCK, KNOCK.

Who's there?

Euripides.

Euripides who?

Euripides jeans, I'm going to be mad.

I'VE BEEN CARRYING THIS HAMMER ALL DAY—NOW MY NECK IS THOR.

I LIKE TO PRETEND MY HEAD IS THOR'S HAMMER. BEWARE, MORTALS!

WHAT DO VIKINGS PUT ON THEIR ROAST BEEF? NORSE RADISH OF COURSE!

OPTICIAN:
Have your eyes
ever been checked
before?
DRAGON:
No, they've always
been red.

Q How did Jack figure out how
many beans to sell his cow for?

A With a cow-culator.

KNOCK, KNOCK? ANYBODY GNOME?

Q What do you get when you cross a **mythical creature** and a **stiletto heel?**

A A shoe-nicorn.

Q Why did Miss Muffet have GPS on her tuffet?

A To keep from losing her whey.

Q What illness do fairy-tale writers get?

A Author-itis.

Did you know that **NASA** sent **ladybugs** and **aphids** into space to see how long the aphids could escape from the ladybugs in **zero gravity?**

Ladybugs are believed to be good luck in many cultures.

RIDDLE ☀ ☀ ME THIS

The **more** that it **appeared**, the **less** Zeus could see. **What was it?**

Darkness.

JACK'S MOTHER:
Why is there always a conversation going on in the garden?
JACK'S FATHER:
Because Jack and his beans talk.

Q What do elf teachers give their students?

A Gnome-work.

185

THE THREE LITTLE PIGS WENT OUT FOR DINNER. When the waiter arrived to take their order, the first pig ordered a coffee, the second pig ordered a tea, and the third pig ordered water.

When the waiter came by again, the first pig ordered soup, the second pig ordered a sandwich, but the third pig ordered another glass of water.

When the waiter returned to take their dessert order, the first pig ordered pie, the second pig ordered cake, and the third pig ordered yet another glass of water.

"Excuse me," the waiter said to the third pig, "why have you ordered nothing but water all evening?"

The third pig replied, "Well one of us has to wee, wee, wee, all the way home!"

Despite their name, red pandas are actually close relatives of the raccoon.

KNOCK, KNOCK.

Who's there?

Althea.

Althea who?

Althea later, alligator!

Q What did **Cinderella** say when the **photos** she ordered didn't **show up?**

A "Someday my prints will come."

Q What did Little Red Riding Hood say when she saw the wolf wearing sunglasses?

A Nothing. She didn't recognize him.

Q Why was the mermaid riding a seahorse?

A Because she was playing water polo.

ALADDIN: I wish for a fur coat.
GENIE: What fur?
ALADDIN: To keep me warm, that's what fur!

Q **What do you get if you cross Tinkerbell and a peacock?**

A A lovely fairy tail.

Q Why did the Ugly Duckling's parents fly south for the winter?

A Because it was too far to walk.

Q Why did **Rapunzel** go to so many **parties?**

A Because she liked to let her hair down.

Q What do **unicorns** call their **fathers?**

A Pop-corns.

Q How did Robin Hood tie his shoelaces?

A With a long bow.

189

HA! HA! HA! HA! HA! HA! HA! HA! HA!

KNOCK,
KNOCK.

Who's there?

Keith.

Keith who?

If I Keith a frog, will it turn into a prince?

Humboldt penguins can rocket through the water at speeds of 30 miles an hour (48 km/h).

Q

What's brown, furry, and has 12 paws?

A The Three Bears.

Q Where do **ogres** dance?

A At the odd ball.

Q What did the sea monster say to the comedian?

A You're Kraken me up!

GREEK GOD 1: Have you seen any movies about Greek mythology?
GREEK GOD 2: No, are they any good?
GREEK GOD 1: Oh yes! You really Odyssey them.

Q What's gray, wears glass slippers, and weighs more than a car?

A Cinderella-phant.

Q What do **elves** learn in **school**?

A The elf-abet.

Q Why is **Peter Pan always flying?**

A Because he Neverlands.

Q Why didn't Goldilocks eat all of her porridge?

A Because it was un-bear-able.

191

Q What kind of **pet** did **Aladdin** have?

A A flying car-pet.

LAUGHABLE LIST

THE OTHER SEVEN DWARFS:

- ☐ Gassy
- ☐ Blotchy
- ☐ Stinky
- ☐ Wheezy
- ☐ Twitchy
- ☐ Lazy
- ☐ Bill

Q What does **Tom Thumb** drink?

A Condensed milk.

> I AM PUG-SEIDON! DOG OF THE SEA! THAT'S WHY MY HELMET IS MADE OF WATERMELON.

CHICKEN LITTLE:
It's raining! Our picnic will be ruined!
CHICKEN LITTLE'S MOM:
I don't mind a little fowl weather.

GOLDILOCKS:
I bought the *worst* thesaurus yesterday.
BABY BEAR:
Really?
GOLDILOCKS:
Oh yes ... not only is it terrible, it's terrible.

Q

Why won't the Big Bad Wolf ever find Little Red Riding Hood's granny again?

A

Because she's going to be well grandma-flaged.

Did you know that **Poseidon** is the **Greek god** of the sea and the brother of Zeus?

He is usually shown with a three-pronged spear called a trident.

Q

On which **side** of the **house** did Jack grow his **beanstalk?**

A

The outside.

Q

What kind of jokes does a unicorn tell?

A

Corny ones.

DRAGON 1:
I just ate a knight in metal armor.
DRAGON 2:
Oh, I love those. They're crunchy on the outside and chewy on the inside.
DRAGON 1:
I didn't like it. I'm not a fan of canned food.

193

SAY WHAT?

NAME
Prince Charming

FAVORITE ACTIVITY
Styling my hare

FAVORITE DANCE
The Bunny Hop

PET PEEVE
Dust bunnies under the bed

LITTLE RUDE RIDING HOOD NEVER VISITED HER GRANNY.

WHAT IS THE BIG BAD WOLF'S FAVORITE FRUIT? THE THREE LITTLE FIGS.

Rabbits come in all sizes. Some weigh less than a pound (0.5 kg) while other breeds can weigh up to 13 pounds (5.9 kg).

RAPUNZEL DIDN'T WANT LONG HAIR, BUT EVENTUALLY IT GREW ON HER.

195

In both Greek and Egyptian mythology, a snake symbolizes eternity.

KNOCK, KNOCK.

Who's there?
Sarah.
Sarah who?
Sarah giant that lives here?

Q Why did Aladdin's lamp hum?

A Because the genie didn't know the words.

GRRRR ...
I'M THE BIG,
BAD WOLF.
FEAR ME!

Q Which elf is the best singer?

A Elf-is Presley.

RIDDLE ✸ ME THIS

What is **light** as a **feather**, but **Hercules** can't hold it for five minutes?

His breath.

Q How are **Greek towels** labeled?

A His and Her-cules.

Q What did **Poseidon** say to the **sea monster?**

A "What's Kraken?"

Q What kind of footwear does a Greek god wear?

A Tennis Zeus.

HERACLES: All three of Cerberus's heads get along so well!

PERSEPHONE: Yes, they have a special connection.

Q What does a unicorn put on its corn dog?

A Pega-sauce.

Beluga whales can change the shape of their heads by blowing air into their sinuses.

KNOCK, KNOCK.

Who's there?
Open says.
Open says who?
Open says me!

198

Q Where did Humpty Dumty get a manufacturing job?

HUMPTY DUMPTY RESUME

A In an eggplant.

Clumsy clowns crushed the king's crown.

Q What is a unicorn's best friend?

A A corn dog.

Q How do you brush a dragon's teeth?

A Very carefully.

Q What kind of dreams does Goldilocks have?

A Night-bears.

Q What do you call a **pretty person** with a **broom?**

A Sweeping Beauty.

CINDERELLA: I made you a numbered list to take to the grocery store with you. Did you take it?
PRINCE CHARMING: Yes, and I think I picked up everything it said to get.
CINDERELLA: Why do you have so many bags? What did you get?
PRINCE CHARMING: 1 pepper, 2 zucchinis, 3 tea bags, 4 loaves of bread, 5 turkeys, and 6 pumpkins.

Q Why did the Cyclops give up his teaching job?

A Because he only had one pupil.

LOL

MYTHS & FABLES

In earlier versions of the **Rumpelstiltskin fairy tale,** he escapes on a **flying LADLE.**

Half of **Iceland's** population **believe** in the existence of **fairies, elves,** and **trolls** called *HULDUFÓLK.*

GELOS was the **GREEK GOD** of laughter.

In the **1960s, BIGFOOT** was placed on **Russia's ENDANGERED SPECIES** list.

BIG FOOT XING

DUE TO SIGHTINGS IN THE AREA OF A CREATURE RESEMBLING "BIG FOOT" THIS SIGN HAS BEEN POSTED FOR YOUR SAFETY

IN CALIFORNIA, U.S.A., A **PONY** DRESSED AS A **UNICORN** ONCE LED **POLICE** ON AN HOURS-LONG **CHASE.**

APPEARANCES CORN BE DECEIVING.

CHAPTER **8**

Uproarious Dinosaurs

KNOCK, KNOCK.
Who's there?
Dinosaurs.
Dinosaurs who?
No, dinosaurs don't who, they roar.

Fossils aren't always bones. Scientists have discovered fossils of dinosaur footprints, eggs, feathers, and even poop!

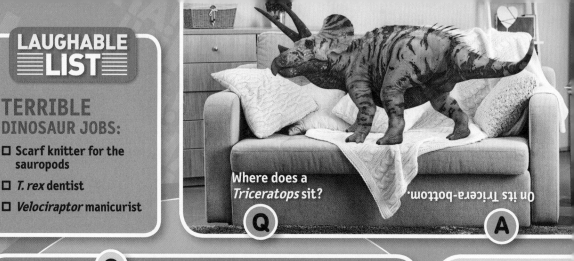

Q Where does a *Triceratops* sit?

A On its Tricera-bottom.

Q What's as BIG as a dinosaur but weighs less than one?

A A dinosaur's shadow.

Q Which swimming dinosaur has the best manners?

PARDON ME, YOU LOOK VERY NICE TODAY.

A The Please-iosaurus.

Did you know that *Diplodocus* was **88 feet** (27 m) **long?** That's almost the **length** of an **NBA basketball court.**

Its neck made up around 20 feet (6 m) of that length.

DINOSAUR 1:
Do you like flying dinosaur puns?
DINOSAUR 2:
No, they are ptero-ble.

TONGUE
TWISTER!

Say this
fast three times:

Diplodocus hocus-pocus.

PACHYCEPHALOSAURUS MOM:
Bring an umbrella to school, it's raining.
PACHYCEPHALOSAURUS KID:
No, I don't want to.
PACHYCEPHALOSAURUS MOM:
Ugh, you have such a hard head.

Q What do you get if you cross a wizard and a *Gigantosaurus*?

IT'S A GOOD THING I'M NOT AFRAID OF HEIGHTS!

A dinosaur-cerer.

A

205

Q Why did tyrannosaurs fight with their teeth?

A Because none of them could win an arm wrestling match.

Q Why did the *Spinosaurus* eat an automobile?

A Because it was a car-nivore.

Q What kind of **dinosaur** is the **fastest?**

A A Pronto-saurus.

PTERODACTYL 1: Can you fly high?
PTERODACTYL 2: I can really saur!

Q What does a dinosaur wear to a wedding?

A A Tricera-top hat.

Q What is a dentist's favorite dinosaur?

A The Flossa-raptor.

Q What kind of dinosaurs like scary movies?

A Terror-dactyls.

Q How did the *Herrerasaurus* feel after its first day at the **gym?**

A Dino-sore.

Q Which **dinosaur** shouldn't **get wet?**

A A Stegosau-rust.

Utahraptor could jump 15 feet (5 m) high even though it weighed as much as a polar bear.

KNOCK, KNOCK.

Who's there?
Ammonia.
Ammonia who?
Ammonia small raptor compared to you!

208

KNOCK, KNOCK.

Who's there?

Micropachycephalosaurus.

Micropachycephalosaurus who?

Seriously? Do you know more than one *Micropachycephalosaurus?*

Despite having the longest name of any dinosaur, *Micropachycephalosaurus* was one of the smallest dinos of them all. It was only 3.3 feet (1 m) long.

Q Why did the dinosaur paint itself different colors?

A So it could hide in a crayon box.

Q Why did *Allosaurus* eat its food raw?

A Because it didn't know how to cook.

Q What do you get when a dinosaur **sneezes?**

A Out of the way!

ALLOSAURUS MOM: Ssshhh, your father is sleeping!
ALLOSAURUS KID: I know, I can hear the dino-snores.

Q Where do dinosaurs sunbathe?

A At the dino-shore.

Q What do you get if you cross a termite and an *Ankylosaurus?*

A Dino-mite.

TONGUE TWISTER!

Say this fast three times:

Ornithomimus is behind us.

HAVE I GOT ANYTHING STUCK IN MY TEETH?

Q What do you get if you cross a mythical flying horse and a spiky dinosaur?

A A Pega-saurus.

209

NAME Nibbler

FAVORITE ACTIVITY
Snacking on the run

FAVORITE FOOD
Anything I can sink
my teeth into

PET PEEVE Flossing

DINOSAUR
PUNS ARE
PTER-ABLE!

The name *Spinosaurus*
means "spine lizard."
Spinosaurus was the
largest carnivorous
dinosaur on Earth.

WHERE
DOES AN
APATOSAURUS
EAT?
ANYWHERE IT
WANTS TO.

WHAT'S BETTER THAN A TALKING DINOSAUR? A SPELLING BEE.

WHAT DO YOU CALL SOMEONE WHO PUTS THEIR RIGHT HAND IN A RAPTOR'S MOUTH? A LEFTY.

WHAT KIND OF DINO CAN YOU RIDE AT A RODEO? A BRONCO-TAURUS.

KNOCK, KNOCK.

Who's there?

Allosaurus.

Allosaurus who?

Allosaurus! 'Ow you doin' today?

Q What do you call a *Velociraptor* in **high heels?**

A My-feet-are-saurus.

Q What's the **difference** between a *Conchoraptor* and a **carrot?**

A A carrot is orange.

NO BONES ABOUT IT, EXTINCTION IS THE PITS.

Q What's **green** and **hangs** from **trees?**

A Dinosaur snot.

KID: Why are all these dinosaur bones so old?
TEACHER: I guess they can't afford new ones.
KID: Will they ever get more bones?
TEACHER: That remains to be seen.

THE *T. REX* FAMILY:

☐ Nervous rex: scared to ride the big roller coasters

☐ T. wrecks: destroys every toy he gets

☐ Tea rex: refuses to drink coffee

☐ Tyrannosaurus flex: loves to go to the gym but usually skips arm days

RIDDLE ✸ ME THIS

What is easy for a baby *Brachiosaurus* to get into, but difficult to get out of?

Trouble.

Did you know that although the name means **"three-horned face,"** *Triceratops* had only **two proper horns?**

The third "horn" was made out of soft proteins, and scientists aren't sure what its purpose was.

DINOSAUR 1: Who stepped on your foot?
DINOSAUR 2: See that *Apatosaurus* over there?
DINOSAUR 1: Yes.
DINOSAUR 2: Well, I didn't.

Q What do you get if you cross a dinosaur and a mouse?

Giant holes in your baseboards.

A

213

A FATHER AND SON BRACHIOSAURUS were eating dinner one day and the son asked, "Dad, are we herbivores?"

"Yes, son. Now eat your dinner," his father replied.

"But if we are herbivores, that means we don't eat bugs, right?" the son asked.

The father sighed, "Yes, son, we don't eat bugs—only plants. Now stop asking questions and eat your dinner."

"But, Dad, are you SURE we don't eat bugs? Are there any kinds of bugs we DO eat?" he asked again.

"Listen!" the father yelled. "I've told you already, we don't eat any kind of bug. We can talk about this after we finish our leaves."

After dinner, the father dino asked, "Now, what is it about eating bugs you wanted to ask me?"

"OH, NEVER MIND," the younger dino said. "There was a large beetle on your leaves but it's gone now."

Cats greet each other by touching noses.

KNOCK, KNOCK.

Who's there?
Raptor.
Raptor who?
Raptor presents, I'm ready for the party!

Q Which **dinosaur** was the most trustworthy?

A The *Troodon*.

Q Why did the *Archaeopteryx* catch the worm?

A Because it was an early bird.

Q What do you call a dinosaur with one eye?

A Eye-saur.

Q What makes more noise than one *Iguanodon*?

A Two *Iguanodons*.

Q What game does an *Apatosaurus* and a *Compsognathus* play together?

A Squash.

Q Why didn't the *Argentinosaurus* cross the road?

A Because there weren't any roads back then.

Q What has a **spiked tail**, giant **plates** on its back, and **16 wheels?**

A A *Stegosaurus* on roller skates.

PALEONTOLOGIST 1: Hey! I think I found a dino skeleton!
PALEONTOLOGIST 2: Nope, fossil-arm.

Q Which **dinosaur** never got lost?

A A Map-usaurus.

217

Yangchuanosaurus was discovered by a construction worker in China in the 1970s. Its full name is *Yangchuanosaurus shangyouensis.* What a mouthful!

KNOCK, KNOCK.

Who's there?

Theropod.

Theropod who?

Theropod of gold at the end of the rainbow?

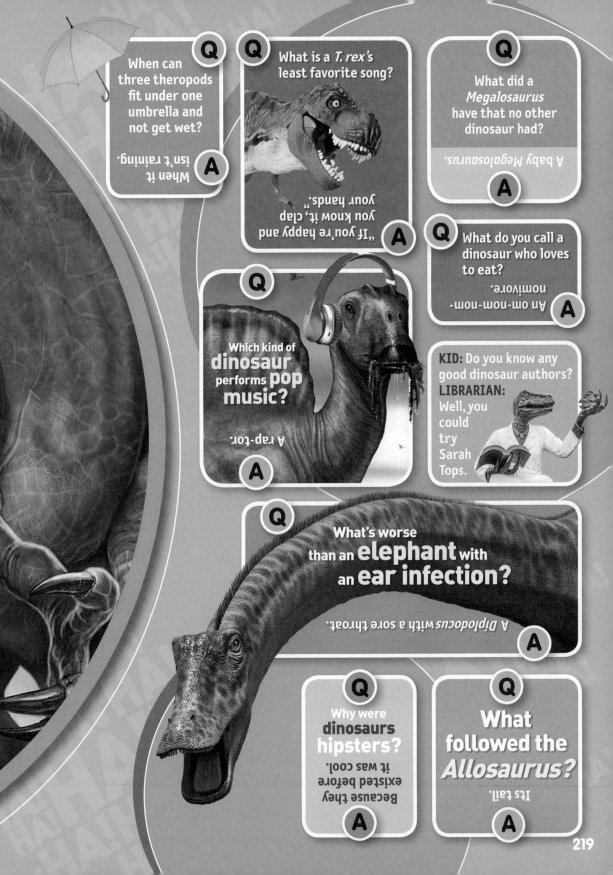

Q When can three theropods fit under one umbrella and not get wet?

A When it isn't raining.

Q What is a *T. rex*'s least favorite song?

A "If you're happy and you know it, clap your hands."

Q What did a *Megalosaurus* have that no other dinosaur had?

A A baby *Megalosaurus*.

Q What do you call a dinosaur who loves to eat?

A An om-nom-nom-nomivore.

Q Which kind of **dinosaur** performs **pop music**?

A A rap-tor.

KID: Do you know any good dinosaur authors?
LIBRARIAN: Well, you could try Sarah Tops.

Q What's worse than an **elephant** with an **ear infection**?

A A *Diplodocus* with a sore throat.

Q Why were **dinosaurs hipsters**?

A Because they existed before it was cool.

Q **What followed the *Allosaurus*?**

A Its tail.

Q

What do you call it when an *Albertosaurus* slides into home plate?

Q

Why are **dinosaur fossils** so **memorable?**

Because they know how to make an impression.

A

ANDERSON:
An *Apatosaurus* just ate a shoe factory!
MIA:
I'm not surprised, they're plant-eaters.

CHIHUAHUA-SAURUS REX STRIKES FEAR IN THE HEARTS OF HUMANS EVERYWHERE!

FOSSIL 1:
How did you meet your wife?
FOSSIL 2:
On a carbon dating site.

RIDDLE ☀ ME THIS

What are **two things** an *Apatosaurus* can **never** eat for **breakfast?**

Lunch and dinner.

A dino-score.

A

Did you know that the **smallest dino** in North America weighed less than a **teacup Chihuahua?**

Fruitadens haagarorum was just 28 inches (71 cm) long and weighed less than two pounds (0.9 kg).

VELOCIRAPTOR 1: I was so hungry I just ate my pillow.
VELOCIRAPTOR 2: I thought you looked a little down in the mouth.

Q

Which plant-eating **dinosaur** can you always find in the **backyard?**

The iguano-lawn.

A

Q

What do you get if you cross a **dinosaur** and a **chicken?**

Tyrannosaurus pecks.

A

SAY WHAT?

NAMES
Spike and Chomper

FAVORITE ACTIVITY
Lurking in swamps

FAVORITE FOOD
Anything chewy

PET PEEVE
Fast food

MY SELFIES NEVER TURN OUT RIGHT.

SHOULD I CALL YOU? OR SEND A TYRANNOSAURUS TEXT?

I'M A LITTLE SHORT-HANDED AT WORK.

T. rex is the most famous of all dinosaurs. It has starred in movies and books as far back as 1918.

I JOINED AN ALL-DINOSAUR SINGING GROUP; IT'S A TYRANNO-CHORUS.

KNOCK, KNOCK.

Who's there?

T. rex.

T. rex who?

There's a T. rex at your door and you want to know its name?!

KNOCK, KNOCK.

Who's there?
Jurassic.
Jurassic who?
If Jurassic you should go lie down.

It's believed that *T. rex* could eat up to 500 pounds (227 kg) of meat in one bite!

RIDDLE ☀ ☀ ME THIS

The **more** a **raptor** takes of these, the **more** it leaves behind. What are they?

Footsteps.

Q Where did the paleontologist find the dinosaur bones?

In a foss-hill.

A

Q What do you get if you cross a **dinosaur** and a **pickle?**

A Dill-ophosaurus.

A

Q What was the most indecisive dinosaur?

The Stay-go-saurus.

A

TONGUE TWISTER!

Say this fast three times:

Spinosaurus **sleeps seven** solid hours.

DAVE: What family does the *T. rex* belong to?
MAGGIE: I don't think families in our neighborhood have one.

Q Why can't you hear a **pterosaur** using the **bathroom?**

Because the *p* is silent.

A

I REALLY KNOW HOW TO MAKE A GREAT IMPRESSION.

PORT-O-DON

PORT-O-DON

KNOCK, KNOCK.

Who's there?
Dino.
Dino who?
Dino you from
somewhere?

Q Why was the *Stegosaurus* such a good volleyball player?

A Because it could really spike the ball.

Q What do you get if you cross a pig and a *Brachiosaurus*?

A Jurassic Pork.

Q What's a *T. rex's* least favorite exercise?

A Push-ups.

Oviraptor's name means "egg stealer" although it has been proved that it wasn't an egg thief at all.

RIDDLE ME THIS

Why could **dinosaurs** go eight days **without** sleeping?

Because they slept at night.

PABLO: I lost my *Apatosaurus*.
SAMI: Why don't you put an ad in the newspaper?
PABLO: Don't be silly, dinosaurs can't read.

LOST DINO

TAG! YOU'RE IT!

Q How do you greet a large **theropod?**

A "Allosaurus!"

Q What do you call a **paleontologist** who **sleeps** all the time?

A Lazy bones.

227

LOL DINOSAURS

There is a town in Colorado, U.S.A., called **Dinosaur.** Some of its STREET NAMES include STEGOSAURUS FREEWAY and TYRANNOSAURUS TRAIL.

Rhinorex was named for its **giant schnoz.** Its name is Latin for **"KING NOSE."**

Paleontologists were SO ANNOYED while trying to RECONSTRUCT the FOSSILIZED HEAD of a newly discovered dinosaur that they named the dino **Irritator.**

ARE WE THERE YET?

Sauropods, or **long-necked dinosaurs,** are believed to have **PASSED GAS** constantly.

I NEVER FALL BEHIND ON MY SCHOOLWORK.

WHEN **STEGOSAURUS** WAS DISCOVERED, **SCIENTISTS** THOUGHT IT HAD A **SECOND BRAIN** IN ITS **REAR END.**

CHAPTER 9

Amusing Music

A cat trainer from Chicago, U.S.A., has formed an all-cat rock band called the Rock-Cats. They are a part of a feline troupe made up of 14 purr-forming cats called the Acro-Cats.

KNOCK, KNOCK.

Who's there?

Harmony.

Harmony who?

Harmony times are you going to make me knock on this door?

Q

How do **composers** remember what to get at the **grocery store?**

A They write a Chopin list.

LAUGHABLE LIST

TERRIBLE BAND NAMES:

- ☐ The Do-You-Think-They-Can-Hear-Us Trio
- ☐ Tone Deaf and the Pitches: an a cappella group
- ☐ Rusty Trumpet and the Squeakers
- ☐ Wind and the Tooter: a bagpipe and horn duet

TRACEY: I was going to tell you a joke about composers but I'm afraid you can't Handel it.
CATHIE: Call me Bach if you change your mind.

LET'S TRY THIS AGAIN FROM THE TOP ...

WE REALLY WANT TO SHOW THEM HOW WELL WE CAN DO THE CHICKEN DANCE.

Q Why are snakes naturally musical?

A Because they have scales.

TONGUE TWISTER!

Say this fast three times:

A tutor who **tooted** the flute, tried to **tutor** two **tooters** to **toot.**

Q Why didn't the wolf want to sing in a band?

A He only knew how to howl.

Did you know that **scientists** have developed technology that analyzes the **sounds** that **chickens** make?

The software can determine the difference between the calls of healthy and sick birds.

ROBERTO: Did you hear about the grizzly that was booed off the stage at the open mic night?
GARRY: No! Was he any good?
ROBERTO: His singing was unbearable.

Q What do you get if you cross an origami teacher and a singer?

A Rapping paper.

Q What is a **composer's** favorite **vegetable?**

A Bach-choy.

233

Q What's a skeleton's favorite instrument?

A The trom-bone.

Q How do you **catch** a **bassoon?**

A With a clari-net.

Q What do you call a dad who raps?

A A hip-pop.

Q What kind of germs do you find in a composer's fridge?

A Bach-teria.

Q Why did the **singer break into song?**

A Because she couldn't find the key.

Q What do you get if you cross a sweet potato and a musician?

A A yam session.

MUSIC TEACHER: Billy, why are you bringing a ladder to our singing lesson?
BILLY: To help me reach the high notes.

Q What has a **trunk,** lots of **keys,** and **four legs?**

A A piano stuck in a tree.

Q What kind of band can't play music?

A A rubber band.

Q What's a golfer's favorite type of music?

A Swing.

234

KNOCK, KNOCK.

Who's there?
Sing.
Sing who?
Whooooooooo!

De Brazza's monkeys have excellent hiding skills, which makes getting an accurate count of how many live in the wild very difficult.

KNOCK, KNOCK.

Who's there?

Arthur.

Arthur who?

Arthur any earplugs
around? This band
is terrible.

Q What kind of music do mummies perform?

A Wrap.

Q What song do you sing at a snowman's birthday party?

A "Freeze a Jolly Good Fellow."

Q What kind of candy plays in the horn section of the orchestra?

MUSIC TEACHER: Please tune in your homework.
HIRO: I don't have it, I forgot my notebook.
MUSIC TEACHER: Now you're really in treble.
HIRO: I know, it wasn't very clef-er of me.

Q What is Tarzan's favorite Christmas song?

A "Jungle Bells."

A A tooty fruity.

Giraffes can grow to be 18 feet (6 m) tall. You don't want this guy standing in front of you at a concert!

OOOO ... I LOVE BELTING OUT MY FAVORITE SONG!

Q What keeps jazz musicians on Earth?

A Groovity.

Q Why did the turkey join the rock band?

A Because he had the drumsticks.

MUSIC HISTORIAN: The composer Handel didn't ever go shopping.
STUDENT: Why not?
MUSIC HISTORIAN: Because he was baroque.

237

NAME
Lionel

FAVORITE HANGOUT
Mane Street

FAVORITE BAND
The Catstreet Boys

PET PEEVE
Copycats

IF A FISH CAN'T SING, THEY CAN USE AUTO-TUNA.

BARITONES BRING ME DOWN.

I LIKE TO SING SOPRANO— IT LEAVES MY LISTENERS ON A HIGH NOTE.

An adult male lion's roar can be heard from five miles (8 km) away. He definitely doesn't need a microphone to sing.

Q What **instrument** do you keep in the **bathroom?**

A A toilet paper tuba.

Q Which pet makes the most noise?

A A trum-pet.

What **instrument** can be **played** and **heard** but **never seen?**

Your voice.

Q What do you call a **lizard** that likes **hip-hop** music?

A A rap-tile.

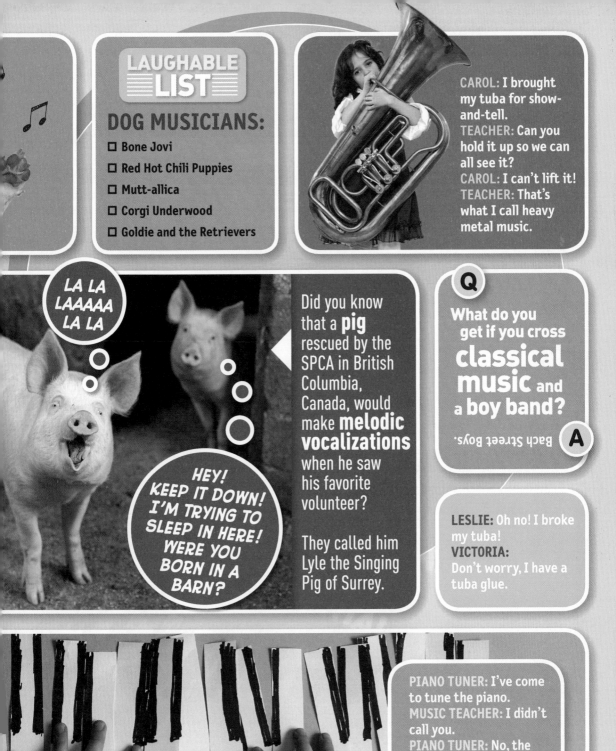

LAUGHABLE LIST

DOG MUSICIANS:

☐ Bone Jovi
☐ Red Hot Chili Puppies
☐ Mutt-allica
☐ Corgi Underwood
☐ Goldie and the Retrievers

CAROL: I brought my tuba for show-and-tell.
TEACHER: Can you hold it up so we can all see it?
CAROL: I can't lift it!
TEACHER: That's what I call heavy metal music.

LA LA LAAAAA LA LA

HEY! KEEP IT DOWN! I'M TRYING TO SLEEP IN HERE! WERE YOU BORN IN A BARN?

Did you know that a **pig** rescued by the SPCA in British Columbia, Canada, would make **melodic vocalizations** when he saw his favorite volunteer?

They called him Lyle the Singing Pig of Surrey.

Q
What do you get if you cross **classical music** and **a boy band?**

A Bach Street Boys.

LESLIE: Oh no! I broke my tuba!
VICTORIA: Don't worry, I have a tuba glue.

PIANO TUNER: I've come to tune the piano.
MUSIC TEACHER: I didn't call you.
PIANO TUNER: No, the people who live next door did.

A BIOLOGY TEACHER TAKES HIS DAUGHTER TO HER ORGAN PERFORMANCE.

When it's her turn to play, she walks out on stage, turns to the audience, and says, "I'd like to thank my father for teaching me everything I know. He is so talented and I'd love for him to perform with me."

Her father is touched and runs up on stage with her.

As the girl starts to play, her father takes a deep breath and begins to shout, "Kidney! Lung! Heart! Spleen! Liver!"

The daughter stops playing and whispers, "Dad! What are you doing?!"

Her father replies, "I thought you said this was an organ recital?"

KNOCK, KNOCK.

Who's there?
Allison.
Allison who?
Allison to the music on the radio.

A zoo in Australia released a music single created by an orangutan named Kluet. The song was recorded on a smartphone music app.

244

Q What do **composers** take when they have a **sore throat?**

A Tchi-cough-sky drops.

Q What do you get if you put a radio in the freezer?

A Cool music.

Q What song did one octopus sing to the other?

A "I wanna hold your hand, hand, hand, hand, hand, hand, hand."

Q Why are **pianos hard** to **open?**

A Because the keys are inside.

Q Why did the girl decide to become an opera singer?

A Because the opera-tunity came up.

Q What **instrument** does a **fisherman** play?

A The bass guitar.

Q What do you do if you **can't find** someone to **sing with?**

A Duet yourself.

FARMER 1:
I taught my horse to play the violin.
FARMER 2:
Is she good at it?
FARMER 1:
She sure is, she's going to be in a musical!
FARMER 2:
Which one?
FARMER 1:
Fiddler on the Hoof.

Q What is a trombone's favorite playground equipment?

A The slide.

245

KNOCK, KNOCK.

Who's there?

Cymbals.

Cymbals who?

Cymbals have horns and others don't.

A female snowy owl will sit on her eggs for a month until they hatch. A male snowy owl will bring her food during this time.

Q What is Beethoven's favorite fruit?

A Ba-na-na-naaa.

Q Why did the pianist bang the side of his head against the keys?

A He wanted to play by ear.

OPERA SINGER 1: Why did you jump in the ocean with your dress on?
OPERA SINGER 2: Because I'm a deep C diva!

I'M NOT READY FOR OPEN MIC NIGHT! WHAT WAS I THINKING?!

Q What has **40 feet** and **sings**?

A A choir.

Q Why **shouldn't** you trust a **harp?**

A Because sometimes they're lyres.

Q How do you know when a musician has left the house?

A He leaves a note.

RIDDLE ☀ ☀ ME THIS

At the **sound** of me, people sometimes stamp their feet and wave their arms, and sometimes they may **laugh** or **weep. What am I?**

Music.

Q What do composers put on their pizzas?

Mozart-rella cheese.

A

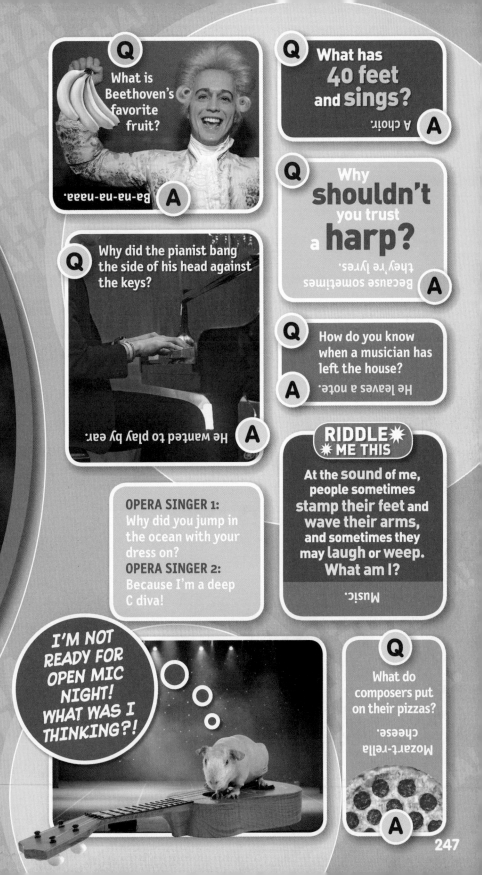

KNOCK, KNOCK.

Who's there?

Tuna.

Tuna who?

Tuna guitar and you can join our band.

Some people listen to dolphin sounds set to music to meditate.

RIDDLE ✲ ME THIS

What is full of keys but can't open any doors?

A piano.

Q Why are icy sidewalks like music?

If you don't C sharp, you'll B-flat. **A**

STEPHEN: Yuck! I was singing in the shower and got shampoo in my mouth.

ANNA: Oh, I love a good soap opera!

Q **What's yellow, weighs 1,000 pounds, and sings?**

Two 500-pound canaries. **A**

Q Why did the kid's tortilla chips start dancing?

Because he put some salsa music on. **A**

MUSICIAN 1: Wow, the conductor is really angry with us.

MUSICIAN 2: He is totally having a tempo-tantrum.

Q What kind of soap does a composer use?

Anti-Bach-terial. **A**

Q **What do you call a musical insect?**

A hum-bug. **A**

I CAN'T READ SHEET MUSIC; I PLAY BY EAR.

SAY WHAT?

NAMES
Rock and Roll

FAVORITE ACTIVITY
Shaking our hips

FAVORITE DANCE
Hippo-Hop

PET PEEVE
Hippo-critical people

THESE JOKES REALLY STRUCK A CHORD.

BE CAREFUL, MUSIC PUNS WILL GET YOU IN TREBLE.

THOSE WHO DON'T LIKE THESE MUSIC PUNS HAVE MY SYMPHONY.

The hippo is considered the third largest land animal (after the white rhino and the elephant).

KNOCK, KNOCK.

Who's there?
Radio.
Radio who?
Radio not, here we come!

I THINK MUSIC JOKES ARE PRETTY SHARP.

NOT IF THEY FALL FLAT.

There are 264 species of monkeys that are divided into two groups: Old World (which live in Africa and Asia) and New World (which live in South America).

KNOCK,
KNOCK.

Who's there?
Turnip.
Turnip who?
Turnip the volume, this is my favorite song!

HMM HMM HMMM ... IF YOU DON'T KNOW THE WORDS, JUST HUM ALONG.

Q What do you call a **musician** who was **petrified by Medusa?**

A A rock star.

Q What do you get if you cross a **lamp** and a **violin?**

A Light music.

RIDDLE ✹ ME THIS

If an **orchestra** is playing outside in a **thunderstorm**, which **member** is most likely to get struck by **lightning?**

The conductor.

Q Why are cats such good singers?

A Because they are naturally mew-sical.

Q What do ghosts bring to their music lessons?

A Sheet music.

Q Why didn't the llama like to perform with a band?

A She enjoyed singing alpaca-pella.

Q Why did the **recliner** learn to play the **guitar?**

A Because it was a rocking chair.

DAD: Why aren't string instruments good at puzzles?
DAUGHTER: I don't know, why?
DAD: Because violins never solve anything.

253

LOL MUSIC

A **SONG** that gets stuck in your **head** is called an **EARWORM.**

A band sent a **piece of pizza** into **SPACE** as part of a **music video.**

The **first musical comedy,** *The Black Domino/ Between You, Me, and the Post,* was performed on **Broadway** in **1878.**

Members of a **marching band** in **Michigan, U.S.A.,** dress as **CLOWNS** while **performing.**

MUSICAL CANINE FREESTYLE

IS A SPORT WHERE **HUMANS** AND **DOGS** PERFORM A ROUTINE TOGETHER. IT COMBINES **DANCE, TRICKS,** AND **OBEDIENCE** TRAINING.

I'M NOT A GREAT DANCER ... I HAVE TWO LEFT FEET.

CHAPTER 10

Riotous Riches

In the 18th century, the value of a coin was determined by its weight in gold or silver. Sometimes a coin would be cut into smaller pieces for payment or to make change.

KNOCK, KNOCK.
Who's there?
Needle.
Needle who?
Needle little help carrying this treasure!

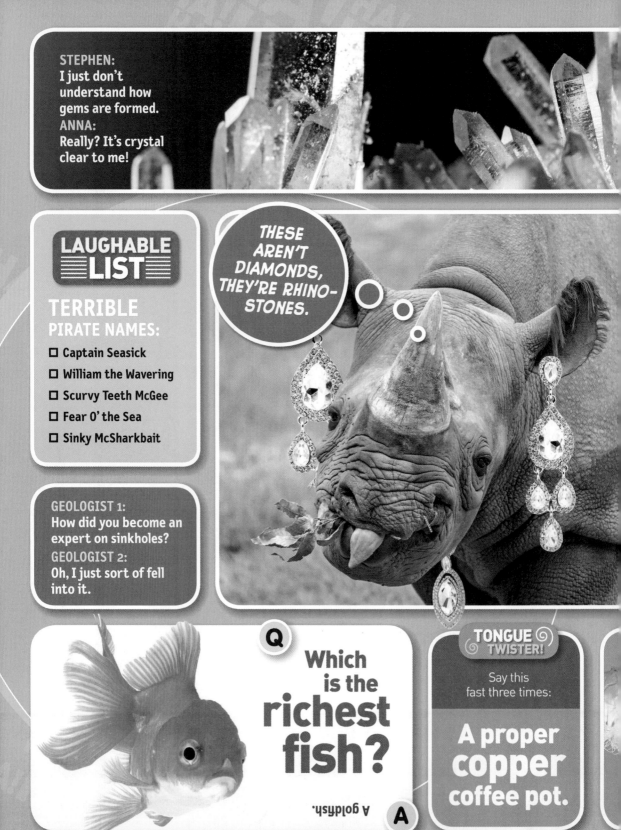

STEPHEN:
I just don't understand how gems are formed.
ANNA:
Really? It's crystal clear to me!

LAUGHABLE LIST

TERRIBLE PIRATE NAMES:

- ☐ Captain Seasick
- ☐ William the Wavering
- ☐ Scurvy Teeth McGee
- ☐ Fear O' the Sea
- ☐ Sinky McSharkbait

THESE AREN'T DIAMONDS, THEY'RE RHINO-STONES.

GEOLOGIST 1:
How did you become an expert on sinkholes?
GEOLOGIST 2:
Oh, I just sort of fell into it.

Q

Which is the **richest fish?**

A goldfish. **A**

TONGUE TWISTER!

Say this fast three times:

A proper **copper** coffee pot.

Q Why did the jewel thief steal a snake from the zoo?

A The sign said it was a diamondback.

Did you know that a **group** of **rhinos** is called a **crash?** Crashes are made up of a female and her calves.

Rhinos are an endangered species. It's estimated there are only around 29,000 of them left in the wild.

Q What's a **pirate's favorite subject** in school?

A Arrrr.

Q What did the pirate say at the end of his 79th year?

A "Aye, Matey."

ARCHAEOLOGIST 1: I just found a tomb of a mummified pharaoh!
ARCHAEOLOGIST 2: Are you serious?
ARCHAEOLOGIST 1: No bones about it!

Q Who did the **archaeologist talk to** when he was **sad?**

A His mummy.

ANCIENT EGYPTIAN 1: Ouch, my back is sore from storing all these treasures in pharaoh's tomb.

ANCIENT EGYPTIAN 2: Maybe you should visit the Cairo-practor.

Q Where do birds invest their money?

A In the stork market.

Q Who stole the **expensive soap** from the **bathtub?**

A The robber duckie.

Q What do you call **money** made of **clay?**

A Play-Dough.

Q What happens when you throw a blue sapphire into the Red Sea?

A It gets wet.

Q Why did the priceless painting go to jail?

A It was framed.

Q Why did the gold prospector call in sick at work?

A He had gold fever.

260

Giant pandas spend about 12 hours of their day eating and can pack away around 25 pounds (11 kg) of bamboo.

KNOCK, KNOCK.

Who's there?

Owen.

Owen who?

I'm Owen you a lot of money. I'll pay you back soon.

KNOCK, KNOCK.

Who's there?

Archie.

Archie who?

Archie-ologists have found some amazing treasures.

A macaw has a bone in its tongue that helps the bird open up fruits and nuts.

Q What do you call it when a dog swallows a wedding ring?

A A diamond in the ruff.

Q Why did the thief take a bath after stealing the royal jewels?

A So he could make a clean getaway.

Q What do you call a pirate who skips school?

A Captain Hooky.

Q What did the **pirate** use to keep his **parrot** on his shoulder?

A Polly-grip.

I'M SURE I CAN DIG UP A GEM OF A JOKE TO TELL YOU. OF QUARTZ, I HOPE IT ISN'T AN EMER-OLD ONE.

PIRATE: Can you take a look at the moles on me back?
DOCTOR: There's nothing to worry about, they're benign.
PIRATE: Shiver me timbers! When I spied them this morning, there be only four!

RIDDLE ME THIS

What has a **head**, a **tail**, no legs, and is **brown**?

A penny.

Q What do you eat to get rich?

A Fortune cookies.

Q What did the robber say when he held up the pizzeria?

A "Gimme all your dough."

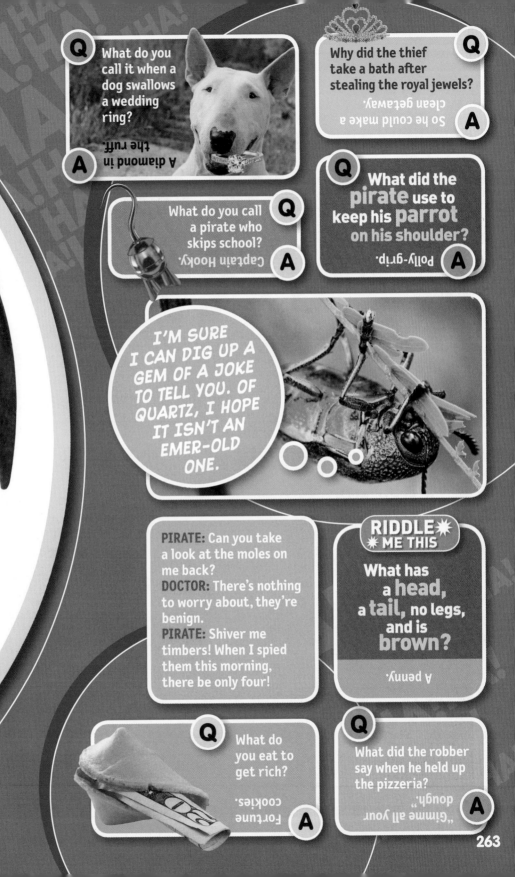

SAY WHAT?

People have been keeping goldfish as pets for more than 2,000 years.

NAMES Goldie, Bubbles, Doubloon, and Bill

FAVORITE ACTIVITY Fishing for compliments

FAVORITE GAME Salmon Says

PET PEEVE Bowls

WE ARE O-FISH-ALLY FABULOUS!

I KEEP MY MONEY IN A RIVERBANK.

IS IT GOLD IN HERE, OR IS IT JUST ME?

BE CAREFUL SWIMMING, YOU DON'T WANT TO FIN-JURE YOURSELF.

KNOCK, KNOCK.

Who's there?
Fission.
Fission who?
Why are there so many fission here?!

Q Why did the pirate buy a baby chick instead of a parrot?

PRICE $1⁰⁰

A Because it was going cheep.

Q Why didn't the **quarter** roll down the hill with the **nickel?**

A Because it had more cents.

RIDDLE ✹ ME THIS

You find some **buried treasure,** but the **more** you **took away,** the **larger** it became. **What is it?**

A hole.

ERICA: I wish I had enough money to buy a yacht.
LISA: What would you do with a yacht?
ERICA: Nothing—I just want enough money to buy one.

LAUGHABLE LIST

HOW TO TELL IF YOUR TREASURE IS FAKE:

☐ Your gold coins have chocolate inside.
☐ Your treasure chest is made of papier-mâché.
☐ Your diamonds bounce.
☐ You were in a toy store when you "discovered" it.
☐ Your diamonds and jewels smell like fruit flavors.

Q

What kind of lipstick do pirates wear?

Ship gloss.

A

Did you know that a **bunny's teeth** never stop growing? They have to chew on wood or hay to keep them **worn down.**

Babies are born with their eyes closed and no fur.

THIS ISN'T THE TYPE OF CARAT I WAS TALKING ABOUT.

SOPHIA:
I'm one step away from being rich!
FRANCESCO:
Really?!
SOPHIA:
Yep, all I need is lots of money!

MUMMY 1:
Wow! Look at all these treasures they buried us with!
MUMMY 2:
Shhh ... let's keep it under wraps.

Q

Why did the man put his money in the freezer?

He wanted some cold hard cash.

A

267

CAPTAIN SHIPWRECK THE PIRATE wrote a letter to his longtime pirate friend, Scurvy McChumbucket:

Dear Scurvy, I've been traveling the sea for many years and have just hauled the largest booty of my life! I have more emeralds and rubies than I can count. I hope you are well, please write to me soon.

Two months passed and his friend didn't respond. Years passed and Shipwreck sent Scurvy many more letters, but he never received a reply.

One day while docked, he spotted Scurvy and rushed over to see him. "Scurvy, my old pirate friend! I'm so happy to see you! I've written you so many letters, but why haven't you responded?"

Scurvy replied, "I prefer to talk aye to aye."

The southern elephant seal is massive! It can grow up to 20 feet (6 m) long and can weigh up to 8,800 pounds (3,992 kg).

KNOCK, KNOCK.

Who's there?
Barry.
Barry who?
Barry the treasure where no one will find it!

Q Why did the baker sell her yeast?

A To make some dough.

Q Why do **bankers go to the movies by themselves?**

A Because they're loaners.

Q What did the ceiling say to the diamond chandelier?

A You light up my life.

Q Why did the spider buy a fancy sports car?

A So he could take it for a spin.

Q Why did the belt go to jail?

A It held up a pair of pants.

Q What does a wasp wear when it goes to the bank to deposit its fortunes?

A A buzz-ness suit.

BUSINESS WOMAN: I have an idea that will double your money instantly.

INVESTOR: Really? Here's $100, what do I do?

BUSINESS WOMAN: Fold it in half.

DO YOU KNOW HOW MUCH CHEESE I CAN BUY WITH THIS?!

Q What's the **most expensive air?**

A A millionaire.

Baby goats can stand within minutes of being born.

KNOCK, KNOCK.

Who's there?

Garden.

Garden who?

Garden these gold coins with my life.

Q What did the solid gold plate say to the jeweled goblet?

A "Dinner's on me."

Q What do you call a **fake Irish diamond?**

A A sham-rock.

Q Where can you see mummies and the treasures of the ancient Egyptian cows?

A At the history moooooseum.

Q When does it rain money?

A If there's a change in the weather.

SCULPTOR: I'll need the diamonds we are embedding into the statue by Thursday.
JEWELER: Can we change it to Friday?
SCULPTOR: Sorry, it's set in stone.

Q Where did the **chandelier** go to **dance?**

A The Crystal Ball.

Q How do you **secure** a **jewelry store?**

A You locket.

Q What did the gold say to the pyrite?

A "You're a fool!"

POLLY'S IN CHARGE NOW! CRACKERS WHENEVER I WANT!

273

Iguanas have a flap of skin under their chins called a dewlap that helps to regulate their body temperature.

KNOCK,
KNOCK.

Who's there?
Jewel.
Jewel who?
Jewel know when I'm here because I'll knock on the door.

Q How much money does a skunk have?

A One scent.

Q What do you call a slug living on a fancy yacht?

A A snail-or.

Q Why did the queen go to the dentist?

A To get crowns on her teeth.

Q Why did the diamond go to the bathroom?

A Because it had to twinkle.

ARCHAEOLOGIST 1: Wow! Look at these cave paintings we found!
ARCHAEOLOGIST 2: Why did cavemen draw so many pictures of hippopotamuses and rhinoceroses on their walls?
ARCHAEOLOGIST 1: Because they couldn't spell the names.

Q Which bird steals from the rich and gives to the poor?

A Robin Hood.

Q Why did the lady buy an **elephant** instead of a **sports car?**

A Because it had a bigger trunk.

Q Why can't a bank keep a secret?

A It has too many tellers.

All kittens are born with blue eyes. They develop eye color at around eight weeks old.

IF MONEY DOESN'T GROW ON TREES, WHY DO BANKS HAVE BRANCHES?

KNOCK, KNOCK.

Who's there?

Nickel.

Nickel who?

Nickel be dropping by for a visit.

Q Why did the oyster keep all of its pearls?

A Because it was shellfish.

Q Where does a shrimp go to sell his diamond necklace?

A The prawn shop.

Q Why did the pirate buy a new ship?

A Because it was on sail.

A GOLDEN EGG! I'M RICH!

Q Why did the employees bring **swimming trunks** and **tennis racquets** to work?

A Because they were headed to mining camp.

RIDDLE ME THIS

A **container** without **hinges, lock,** or **key;** a golden treasure lies inside me. What am I?

An egg.

DAD: Have you found a nice card for Mom yet? You've opened 100 of them so far!
DAUGHTER: I know, I'm looking for one with money inside.

HAPPY:) BIRTHDAY

Q What's valuable, **green,** and **sings?**

A Emerald Presley.

JEWELER: How do you feel about these jewels?
CUSTOMER: My love for jewels is crystal clear!

Q Why did the archaeologist move the Egyptian pyramids closer to the Nile River?

A So they could have a tomb with a view.

River otters can stay underwater for up to eight minutes.

KNOCK, KNOCK.

Who's there?

Money.

Money who?

Money aches from all the stairs I climbed.

LOL RICHES

The term **"FUNNY MONEY"** describes **COUNTERFEIT**, or fake, **money.**

An orange, 10-foot (3-m)-tall metal statue of a **balloon dog** sold at auction for **$142 million!**

The first **American coin**, called the **FUGIO CENT**, was designed by **Benjamin Franklin** and was inscribed **"Mind Your Business."**

A man once **PRANKED treasure hunters** by burying a chest filled with **chocolate gold coins** and **costume jewelry.**

A JEWELER IN HONG KONG BUILT A **$27 MILLION BATHROOM.** THE TOILET AND SINK WERE MADE OF SOLID 24-KARAT GOLD.

JOKE**FINDER**

ILLUSTRATIONCREDITS

Abbreviations: DS = Dreamstime; GI = Getty Images; SS = Shutterstock
Front cover: (UP RT), Pitipat Usanakornkul/SS; (LE), Heinrich van den Berg/GI; (LO RT), Robynrg/SS; **Back cover:** Richard Yoshida/SS; **Spine:** Pitipat Usanakornkul/SS; 1, Seregraff/SS; 2 (UP LE), Grigorita Ko/SS; 2 (UP CTR), Csanad Kiss/SS; 2 (UP RT), photomaster/SS; 2 (CTR LE), Natalia Kirsanova/SS; 2 (CTR), Wiboon Wirat-thanaphan/SS; 2 (CTR RT), effective stock photos/SS; 2 (LO LE), Mark O'Flaherty/SS; 2 (LO CTR), Sandra Standbridge/SS; 2 (LO RT), Turbojet/SS; 3 (UP RT), Pitipat Usanakornkul/SS; 3 (CTR LE), Heinrich van den Berg/GI; 3 (LO RT), Robynrg/SS; 4-5, sniper thaphae/SS; 6-7 (BACKGROUND), Aekawut Rattawan/SS; 6 (LO RT), DR Travel Photo and Video/SS; 7 (CTR), Javier Brosch/SS; 8 (UP RT), Kalamurzing/SS; 8 (CTR LE), anna_pro3/SS; 8 (LO CTR), Smit/SS; 8 (LO CTR RT), Best dog photo/SS; 9 (UP), Blueenayim/DS; 9 (UP CTR LE), (UP CTR), Elnur/SS; 9 (UP RT), Richard Peterson/SS; 9 (CTR), Nadezhda V. Kulagina/SS; 9 (LO LE), FotoYakov/SS; 9 (LO RT), Vyaseleva Elena/SS; 10 (UP LE), Emilia Stasiak/SS; 10 (UP

LE), Draghicich/DS; 10 (UP CTR), David Tadevosian/SS; 10 (UP RT), milart/SS; 10 (UP RT), Winai Tepsuttinun/SS; 10 (CTR LE), Laborant/SS; 10 (CTR LE), Grigorev Mikhail/SS; 10 (CTR RT), Anurak Pongpatimet/SS; 10 (LO LE), Jagodka/SS; 10 (LO CTR), Chaykha.j.s/SS; 10 (LO RT), Africa Studio/SS; 11, Santi Nanta/SS; 12, Grigorita Ko/SS; 13 (UP CTR), Madhourse/SS; 13 (UP CTR RT), Richard Peterson/SS; 13 (UP RT), Robynrg/SS; 13 (CTR RT), Nataliia K/SS; 13 (LO LE), Dora Zett/SS; 13 (LO CTR), Inna Astakhova/SS; 13 (LO RT), Vangert/SS; 14-15, Minerva Studio/SS; 16 (UP LE), vblinov/SS; 16 (UP), Apple's Eyes Studio/SS; 16 (CTR LE), Tsekhmister/SS; 16 (CTR LE), nafterphoto/SS; 16 (CTR RT), Koldunov Alexey/SS; 16 (LO), idreamphoto/SS; 17 (UP LE), Dpullman/SS; 17 (UP CTR), Jan Sommer/SS; 17 (UP RT), Aneta Jungerova/SS; 17 (LO RT), halfmax.ru/SS; 18-19 (BACKGROUND), Trong Nguyen/SS; 18 (LO RT), Mik122/iStockphoto; 19 (CTR RT), Tsekhmister/SS; 19 (LO RT), Prokrida/SS; 20, Eric Isselee/SS; 21 (UP LE), (UP RT), Eric Isselee/SS; 21 (UP CTR), Jak Wonderly/NGS; 21 (UP CTR RT), darkpurplebear/SS; 21 (CTR LE), Noor Haswan Noor Azman/

SS; 21 (CTR), Ivanova N/SS; 21 (CTR RT), effective stock photos/SS; 21 (CTR RT), Dan Kosmayer/SS; 21 (LO LE), eva_blanco/SS; 21 (LO RT), Everita Pane/SS; 22, leisuretime70/SS; 23 (UP CTR), Rommel Canlas/SS; 23 (UP RT), Kurit afshen/SS; 23 (CTR), Andrey Slepov/SS; 23 (CTR RT), Alptraum/DS; 23 (CTR RT), sianc/SS; 23 (LO LE), photomaster/SS; 23 (LO RT), Peyker/SS; 24 (UP LE), PHOTOCREO Michal Bednarek/SS; 24 (LE), prapass/SS; 24 (CTR LE), photomaster/SS; 24 (CTR RT), FIlosofArtFoto/SS; 24 (LO LE), gui jun peng/SS; 24 (LO CTR), Kraska/SS; 25 (UP LE), Karpova/SS; 25 (UP RT), MARKABOND/SS; 25 (CTR RT), dien/SS; 25 (CTR RT), R. Gino Santa Maria/Shutterfree, LLC/DS; 25 (CTR RT), paperglede/SS; 25 (LO LE), Stephen Mcsweeny/SS; 26-27, kuban_girl/SS; 28, Bruce Raynor/SS; 29 (UP RT), fantom_rd/SS; 29 (CTR LE), Markus Mainka/SS; 29 (CTR LE), alptraum/GI; 29 (CTR), WilleeCole Photography/SS; 29 (CTR RT), mikeledray/SS; 29 (CTR RT), David Carillet/SS; 29 (LO LE), serg78/SS; 29 (LO CTR), Eric Isselee/SS; 29 (LO RT), Pakhnyushchyy/DS; 30, Gert Vrey/SS; 31 (UP), Ronnie Chua/SS; 31 (UP CTR), (LO RT), Eric Isselee/SS; 31 (CTR RT), choosangyeon/SS; 31 (CTR RT), Sergey Mironov/SS; 31 (LO CTR), Javier Brosch/SS; 32-33 (BACKGROUND), K Woodgyer/SS; 32 (UP RT), Alexandru Nika/SS; 32 (UP RT), Eric Isselee/SS; 32 (UP RT), sylv1rob1/SS; 32 (LE), Ljupco Smokovski/SS; 32 (CTR LE), Yuliyan Velchev/SS; 32 (CTR LE), Jagodka/SS; 32 (LO LE), photolinc/SS; 32 (LO CTR), Konjushenko Vladimir/SS; 32 (LO RT), Alesandro14/SS; 33 (LO CTR), cynoclub/SS; 33 (LO), Lotus Images/SS; 34-35, teinstud/SS; 35 (UP RT), Tulpahn/SS35 (RT), charles taylor/SS; 35 (LO LE), ThomasVogel/GI; 36 (UP RT), RomanR/SS; 36 (CTR), Kjpargeter/SS; 36 (CTR RT), AnirutKhattirat/SS; 36 (LO), taviphoto/SS; 36 (LO RT), wavebreakmedia/SS; 37 (UP LE), 3Dalia/SS; 37 (UP RT), Haver/SS; 37 (CTR), Grigorita Ko/SS; 37 (LO LE), ifong/SS; 37 (LO LE), Draghicich/DS; 38 (UP LE), Vadim Sadovski/SS; 38 (UP), oksana2010/SS; 38 (UP CTR), Eric Isselee/SS; 38 (CTR LE), kirill_makarov/SS; 38 (CTR LE), Petlia Roman/SS; 38 (CTR), Apostle/SS; 38 (CTR RT), Julien Tromeur/SS; 38 (LO LE), Chad Soeller Photography/SS; 38 (LO RT), Flegere/SS; 39, Donhype/GI; 40, Juniper101/SS; 41 (UP LE), Eric Isselee/SS; 41 (UP CTR RT), (UP RT), Greg and Jan Ritchie/SS; 41 (UP RT), sirius1/SS; 41 (CTR LE), Bakhur Nick/SS; 41 (LO LE), Ultrashock/SS; 41 (LO RT), magnetix/SS; 42-43, reptiles4all/SS; 42 (LO LE), 43 (LO RT), WCephei/GI; 43 (LO RT), EM Karuna/SS44 (UP CTR), nelen/SS; 44 (UP RT), JasminkaM/SS; 44 (CTR LE), Freedom Life/SS; 44 (CTR LE), Inna Ogando/SS; 44 (CTR RT), Liliya Kulianionak/SS; 44 (LO), S.Borisov/SS; 45 (UP CTR), Photodisc; 45 (UP RT), oksankash/SS; 45 (LO RT), Khun mix/SS; 46-47 (BACKGROUND), Phonlamai Photo/SS; 46 (LO LE), Dan Kosmayer/SS; 47 (LO CTR), VladKK/SS; 47 (LO RT), Talaj/SS; 48, Sergey Uryadnikov/SS; 49 (UP CTR), Palto/SS; 49 (UP RT), ljpat/GI; 49 (UP RT), DR-images/SS; 49 (CTR LE), Anettphoto/SS; 49 (CTR), glenda/SS; 49 (CTR RT), Sergey Nivens/SS; 49 (LO RT), Tanya_mtv/SS; 50, Nattakorn Suphatheera/SS; 51 (UP CTR), Palto/SS; 51 (UP RT), Fablok/SS; 51 (CTR RT), Demchyna/SS; 51 (LO LE), Volodymyr Nikitenko/SS; 51 (LO RT), mollicart/SS; 52 (UP), Pashin Georgiy/SS; 52 (CTR LE), Take Photo/SS; 52 (CTR), Wiratchai wansamngam/SS; 52 (LO RT), moritorus/SS; 53 (UP LE), Bella D/SS; 53 (UP LE), Telnov Oleksii/SS; 53 (UP LE), Sonya illustration/SS; 53 (UP CTR), Alexey Filatov/SS; 53 (UP RT), Adam Radosavljevic/SS; 53 (LO RT), Ivan_Nikulin/SS; 54 (FORE-GROUND), Sergey Peterman/SS; 55 (CTR), Damsea/SS; 56, Csanad Kiss/SS; 57 (UP CTR), Gregory Pelt/SS; 57 (UP RT), Haywiremedia/SS; 57 (CTR LE), majo1122331/SS; 57 (CTR), Africa Studio/SS; 57 (LO LE), Relja/SS; 57 (LO CTR), grapestock/SS; 58, Janice Storch/SS; 59 (UP CTR), Andrej Antic/SS; 59 (UP CTR RT), Vladyslav Starozhylov/SS; 59 (CTR), Djomas/SS; 59 (LO CTR), Andrey Eremin/SS; 59 (LO RT), Sashkin/SS; 60-61 (BACKGROUND), K Woodgyer/SS; 60 (UP RT), cougarsan/SS; 60 (CTR LE), Palto/SS; 60 (LO RT), sirikorn thamniyom/SS; 61 (LE), TakaYIB/SS; 61 (LO RT), kirill_makarov/SS; 62-63 (BACKGROUND), Denis Belitsky/SS; 63 (RT), tobkatrina/SS; 64 (UP LE), Pro3DArtt/SS; 64 (UP LE), Ton Bangkeaw/SS; 64 (UP RT), Khadi Ganiev/SS; 64 (UP RT), Tim UR/SS; 64 (LO LE), Loiizallz/SS; 64 (LO LE), Ink Drop/SS; 65 (UP LE), Pachai Leknettip/SS; 65 (CTR LE), mina/SS; 65 (CTR RT), Ivan_Nikulin/SS; 65 (LO LE), luxxxam/SS; 65 (LO LE), Svitlana-ua/SS; 66 (UP LE), Ivan_Nikulin/SS; 66 (UP RT), Burhan Bunardi/SS; 66 (LE), Daniel Thornberg/DS; 66 (CTR LE), Fotomay/SS; 66 (CTR), Olga Lyubkin/SS; 66 (CTR RT), Dudarev Mikhail/SS; 66 (LO LE), Nikita Stepanov/SS; 66 (LO CTR), Sanjacm/SS; 66 (LO LE), Denis Kovin/SS; 67 (UP), Nathapol Kongseang/SS; 67 (CTR), PhotoMediaGroup/SS; 68, reptiles4all/SS; 69 (UP CTR), AS Food studio/SS; 69 (UP CTR), OnlyZoia/SS; 69 (CTR LE), Nathapol Kongseang/SS; 69 (CTR RT), Chokchai Poomichaiya/SS; 69 (LO LE), CrackerClips Stock Media/SS; 69 (LO RT), Vadarshop/SS; 70-71, grafxart/SS; 72 (UP), Ivan_Nikulin/SS; 72 (CTR RT), jurra8/SS; 72 (LO LE), Nattee Chalermtiragool/SS; 72 (LO LE), kuzzie/SS; 73 (UP LE), Room27/SS; 73 (UP RT), Sharon Keating/SS; 73 (LO LE), kuzzie/SS; 73 (LO CTR), lady-luck/SS; 73 (LO CTR RT), Arkadiusz Fajer/SS; 73 (LO RT), Melica/SS; 74-75 (BACKGROUND), KPG_Payless/SS; 74 (LE), rangizzz/SS; 74 (LO LE), Mauhorng/DS; 75 (CTR RT), kariphoto/SS; 75 (CTR RT), Kitch Bain/SS; 75 (LO RT), bokan/SS; 76, Armando Frazao/SS; 77 (UP CTR), Jason Newcomb/SS; 77 (UP CTR), photo5963_shutter/SS; 77 (CTR LE), Ivonne Wierink/SS; 77 (CTR), art_of_sun/SS; 77 (CTR), Tiger Images/SS; 77 (CTR RT), Miyu Nur/SS; 77 (LO LE), Alongkorn Sanguansook/SS; 77 (LO RT), Dmitry Kalinovsky/SS; 78, sivilla/SS; 79 (UP CTR), Master1305/SS; 79 (UP RT), Azuzl/SS; 79 (CTR), Lightspring/SS; 79 (CTR), Nathapol Kongseang/SS; 79 (LO CTR), pryzmat/SS; 79 (LO RT), Ivan_Nikulin/SS; 80 (UP LE), desk006/SS; 80 (UP CTR LE), (UP RT), dashadima/SS; 80 (CTR RT), Christin Lola/SS; 80 (LO), Africa Studio/SS; 81 (UP LE), Viktorija Reuta/SS; 81 (UP LE), Pri Ma/SS; 81 (UP LE), kuzzie/SS; 81 (UP RT), Potapov Alexander/SS; 81 (UP RT), SS; 81 (UP RT), WilleeCole Photography/SS; 81 (CTR), rudall30/SS; 81 (LO RT), beerblur/SS; 82-83, awdebenham/SS; 84, SasinTipchai/SS; 85 (UP LE), Abdie/SS; 85 (UP LE), Inked Pixels/SS; 85 (UP RT), guentermanaus/SS; 85 (CTR LE), Marietjie/SS; 85 (CTR), Marcin Sylwia Ciesielski/SS; 85 (CTR RT), Kjpargeter/SS; 85 (CTR RT), Nataliia Pyzhova/SS; 85 (LO CTR), Paul Looyen/SS; 85 (LO CTR), Derek Brumby/SS; 85 (LO RT), Atomazul/SS; 86, Wiboon Wiratthanaphan/SS; 87 (UP LE), NatUlrich/SS; 87 (UP CTR), Zmiter/SS; 87 (UP CTR RT), Hurst Photo/SS; 87 (CTR LE), Narucha Klinudom/SS 87 (LO LE), 3d_man/SS; 87 (LO LE), RikoBest/SS; 87 (LO CTR), Ratchat/SS; 87 (LO RT), sruilk/SS; 88-89 (BACKGROUND), K Woodgyer/SS; 88 (UP RT), Africa Studio/SS; 88 (LO LE), Julia Kopacheva/SS; 88 (LO RT), Isselee/DS; 89 (LO LE), George Rose/GI; 89 (LO RT), Inspired By Maps/SS; 90-91 (BACKGROUND), Irina Chyda/SS; 91 (UP), vitaliy_73/SS; 91 (UP CTR), Lilkin/SS; 91 (CTR), Sonsedska Yuliia/SS; 91 (LO CTR), 3DMI/SS; 92 (UP CTR), Billion Photos/SS; 92 (CTR), Vereshchagin Dmitry/SS; 92 (LO LE), Dudarev Mikhail/SS; 92 (LO CTR), aleksander hunta/SS; 93 (UP LE), blacklightdistrict/SS; 93 (UP CTR), A StockStudio/SS; 93 (CTR LE), dibrova/SS; 93 (LO CTR), Tercer Ojo Photography/SS; 93 (LO RT), Muzhik/SS; 93 (LO RT), Africa Studio/SS; 94 (UP LE), Jacek Chabraszewski/SS; 94 (UP CTR), Africa Studio/SS; 94 (CTR), Jak Wonderly/NGS; 94 (RT), marekuliasz/SS; 94 (LO LE), Sky Antonio/SS; 94 (LO CTR), aguiters/SS; 94 (LO RT), Shirstok/SS; 95, emoraes/SS; 96, Sandra Standbridge/SS; 97 (UP CTR), Oleksii Sidorov/SS; 97 (UP CTR), Khunaspix/DS; 97 (UP RT), Onsunee/SS; 97 (UP RT), Image Ideas; 97 (UP RT), Dragance137/SS; 97 (LO LE), kataleewan intarachote/SS; 97 (LO RT), EgudinKa/SS; 98-99, David & Micha Sheldon/GI; 100 (UP CTR), the palms/SS; 100 (UP CTR), Anthony Feoutis/SS; 100 (LE), Rick Becker-Leckrone/SS; 100 (CTR), Mezhetskaia Valentina/SS; 100 (LO LE), Issarawat Tattong/SS; 100 (LO RT), a_v_d/SS; 101 (UP LE), charles taylor/SS; 101 (UP CTR), seaonweb/SS; 101 (UP RT), iidea studio/SS; 101 (LO RT), wavebreakmedia/SS; 102-103 (BACKGROUND), Victor Lapaev/SS; 102 (LO RT), Anan Kaewkhammul/SS; 103 (LO RT), Susan Schmitz/SS; 104, FCG/SS; 105 (UP CTR), Billion Photos/SS; 105 (UP CTR), Revel Pix LLC/SS; 105 (UP RT), Cesare Palma/SS; 105 (CTR), Eric Isselee/SS; 105 (CTR), Africa Studio/SS; 105 (CTR), Zeljko Radojko/SS; 105 (RT), Kristina Landina/SS; 105 (LO CTR LE), Iryna Kuznetsova/SS; 105 (LO LE), Mark William Penny/SS; 105 (LO RT), Tony Campbell/SS; 106, Sergey Uryadnikov/SS; 107 (UP CTR), Vitalii Nesterchuk/SS; 107 (UP RT), Kim Howell/SS; 107 (CTR RT), Evgeny Prokofyev/SS; 107 (LO LE), Yellowj/SS; 107 (LO CTR), Glenn Young/SS; 107 (LO RT), Paya Mona/SS; 108 (UP), antb/SS; 108 (CTR LE), Laborant/SS; 108 (CTR LE), Amplion/SS; 108 (CTR LE), Ksander/SS; 108 (CTR), Josh Schutz/SS; 108 (LO LE), NAPA/SS; 108 (LO LE), kariphoto/SS; 109 (UP CTR), Andrey_Popov/SS; 109 (UP RT), ohrim/SS; 109 (CTR), Heather L. Hubbard/SS; 109 (LO LE), Africa Studio/SS; 109 (LO LE), Alexander Raths/SS; 110-111, Mario_Hoppmann/SS; 112, Dennis Donohue/DS; 113 (UP CTR), Elnur/SS; 113 (UP RT), Olhastock/SS; 113 (UP RT), W. Scott McGill/SS; 113 (CTR LE), sumire8/SS; 113 (CTR), Sergey Nivens/SS; 113 (LO LE), ilterriorm/SS; 113 (LO LE), Alexander Raths/SS; 113 (LO RT), Hortimages/SS; 113 (LO RT), Andrey_Popov/SS; 114, Mark O'Flaherty/SS; 115 (UP LE), Twin Design/SS; 115 (UP CTR), whanlamoon/SS; 115 (UP CTR), photomaster/SS; 115 (CTR), michelangeloop/SS; 115 (RT), Albo003/SS; 115 (LO CTR), Leena Robinson/SS; 116-117 (BACKGROUND), K Woodgyer/SS; 116 (UP RT), Maceofoto/SS; 116 (CTR RT), sergign/SS; 116 (LO LE), Paul A. Souders/GI; 116 (LO RT), SizeSquare's/SS; 117 (CTR), Nerthuz/SS; 117 (LO), Kovalenko Alexander/SS; 118-119 (BACKGROUND), mirtmirt/SS; 119 (CTR), Javier Brosch/SS; 120 (UP), Amplion/SS; 120 (UP CTR LE), Mark52/SS; 120 (CTR), cgsawma/SS; 120 (LO LE), Anastasia_Panait/SS; 120 (LO CTR LE), Tom Bird/SS; 120 (LO CTR), Derek Brumby/SS; 121 (UP), timquo/SS; 121 (CTR RT), Carola Schubbel/DS; 121 (LO LE), Vitalina Rybakova/SS; 121 (LO CTR LE), titov dmitriy/SS; 122 (UP LE), E. O./SS; 122 (UP CTR), rzstudio/SS; 122 (UP RT), Kelvin Wong/SS; 122 (CTR LE), Eric Isselee/SS; 122 (CTR LE), Africa Studio/SS; 122 (CTR RT), Jiang Hongyan/SS; 122 (LO LE), geertweggen/SS; 122 (LO CTR RT), HarisEna/SS; 123, Helen E. Grose/SS; 124, Adrian Dubler/SS; 125 (UP), Photo wolf/SS; 125 (UP CTR), nikkytok/SS; 125 (UP RT), Photo Image/SS; 125 (CTR), Joe Belanger/SS; 125 (LO CTR), Alexander Chaikin/SS; 126-127, pchoui/GI; 128 (UP), Alextype/SS; 128 (CTR LE), prokopphoto/SS; 128 (LO), imdproduction/SS; 129 (UP), Teim/SS; 129 (LE), Stanimir G.Stoev/SS; 129 (RT), Image Source; 129 (LO), SC Image/SS; 130-131 (BACK-GROUND), acid2728k/SS; 130 (LO RT), Shariff Che'Lah/DS; 131 (LO), Rajesh Narayanan/SS; 132, Imageman/SS; 133 (UP CTR), Irina Kozorog/SS; 133 (UP RT), Hivaka/SS; 133 (CTR LE), Oksana Mizina/SS; 133 (CTR), Oleg Senkov/SS; 133 (CTR RT), kamnuan/SS; 133 (LO RT), NaughtyNut/SS; 134, gabigaasenbeek/SS; 135 (UP LE), Peshkova/SS; 135 (UP CTR), NaughtyNut/SS; 135 (CTR), Africa Studio/SS; 135 (CTR), ollirg/SS; 135 (CTR RT), Kletr/SS; 135 (LO LE), 33333/SS; 135 (LO CTR), Rich Carey/SS; 135 (LO RT), Pixeljoy/SS; 136 (UP LE), Netfalls Remy Musser/SS; 136 (CTR LE), Africa Studio/SS; 136 (RT), Milkovasa/SS; 136 (LO LE), Kletr/SS; 136 (LO CTR LE), S.Borisov/SS; 136 (LO RT), Eric Isselee/SS; 137 (UP RT), vvoe/SS; 137 (LO), Andrew Paul Deer/SS; 138-139, JoffreyM/SS; 140, erikjohnphotography/SS; 141 (UP CTR), exopixel/SS; 141 (UP CTR RT), MidoSemsem/SS; 141 (UP RT), Elnur/SS; 141 (CTR), Mads Hjorth Jakobsen/SS; 141 (CTR RT), Voronin76/SS; 141 (RT), Kletr/SS; 141 (LO LE), Go Exploring/SS; 141 (LO CTR RT), JIANG HONGYAN/SS; 141 (LO RT), Leonard Zhukovsky/SS; 142, Astroette/SS; 143 (UP RT), its_al_dente/SS; 143 (CTR), Suksamran1985/SS; 143 (LO CTR), Romaset/SS; 144-145 (BACKGROUND), K Woodgyer/SS; 144 (UP RT), Philm04/SS; 144 (CTR LE), srisakorn wonglakorn/SS; 144 (LO CTR), NATALIA61/SS; 144 (LO CTR), Katflare/SS; 144 (LO RT), DiversityStudio/SS; 145 (UP CTR), melissa held/SS; 145 (LO CTR), nexus 7/SS; 145 (LO), Digital Genetics/SS; 146-147 (BACKGROUND), Irina Kozorog/SS; 146 (UP RT), 147 (UP LE), Brand X Pictures; 147 (CTR), ND700/SS; 147 (CTR), David Carillet/SS; 148 (UP RT), Szczepan Klejbuk/SS; 148 (CTR RT), Scarabaeus/SS; 148 (LO CTR), t_kimura/GI; 148 (LO CTR), spaxiax/SS; 148 (LO RT), Tsekhmister/SS; 148 (LO RT), Halfpoint/SS; 149 (UP LE), Nor Gal/SS; 149 (UP RT), Kurit afshen/SS; 149 (UP RT), ajt/SS; 149 (CTR

Since 1888, the National Geographic Society has funded more
than 12,000 research, exploration, and preservation projects
around the world. The Society receives funds from National
Geographic Partners, LLC, funded in part by your purchase.
A portion of the proceeds from this book supports this vital
work. To learn more, visit natgeo.com/info.

NATIONAL GEOGRAPHIC and Yellow Border Design are
trademarks of the National Geographic Society, used
under license.

For more information, visit nationalgeographic.com,
call 1-800-647-5463, or write to the following address:

National Geographic Partners
1145 17th Street N.W.
Washington, D.C. 20036-4688 U.S.A.

Visit us online at nationalgeographic.com/books

For librarians and teachers: ngchildrensbooks.org

More for kids from National Geographic:
natgeokids.com

National Geographic Kids magazine inspires children
to explore their world with fun yet educational articles
on animals, science, nature, and more. Using fresh
storytelling and amazing photography, *Nat Geo Kids*
shows kids ages 6 to 14 the fascinating truth about
the world—and why they should care.
kids.nationalgeographic.com/subscribe

For information about special discounts for bulk
purchases, please contact National Geographic Books
Special Sales: specialsales@natgeo.com

For rights or permissions inquiries, please
contact National Geographic Books Subsidiary
Rights: bookrights@natgeo.com

The publisher would like to thank the following people
for making this book possible: Kate Hale, executive editor;
Michaela Weglinski, editorial assistant; Callie Broaddus,
senior designer; Sarah J. Mock, senior photo editor;
Joan Gossett, editorial production manager; Molly Reid,
production editor; and Anne LeongSon and Gus Tello, design
production assistants.

Design, Editorial, and Production by
Plan B Book Packagers

Trade paperback ISBN: 978-1-4263-3168-8
Reinforced library binding ISBN: 978-1-4263-3169-5

Printed in China
18/RRDS/1